M000095490

shortcuts to success

home cooking

Silvana Franco

photography by Gus Filgate

First published in the UK in 2003 by Quadrille Publishing Limited
Alhambra House 27-31 Charing Cross Road London WC2H OLS

This edition published by Silverback Books, Inc., San Francisco, California. www.silverbackbooks.com

Editorial director Jane O'Shea **Creative director** Helen Lewis
Managing editor Janet Illsley **Art direction** Vanessa Courtier
Editor Norma MacMillan **Designer** Sue Storey **Photographer** Gus Filgate
Food stylist Silvana Franco **assisted by** Anna-Lisa Aldridge
Props stylist Jane Campsie **Production** Vincent Smith and Jane Rogers

Text © 2003 Silvana Franco Photography © 2003 Gus Filgate
Design and layout © 2003 Quadrille Publishing Limited

Cataloging in Publication Data: a catalog record for this book is available from the British Library.

ISBN 1-930603-09-6
Printed in China

contents

NOTES

Measurements are in standard American cups and spoons.

Use fresh herbs unless dried herbs are suggested.

Use freshly ground black pepper unless otherwise stated.

Eggs from cage-free or free-range hens are recommended, and extra large eggs should be used except where a different size is specified.

Recipes that feature raw or lightly cooked eggs should be avoided by vulnerable people (anyone who is pregnant, babies and young children, the elderly, and those who are sick or who have compromised immune systems), unless using eggs that have been pasteurized in shell.

introduction

Mealtimes in my home have never followed a pattern. Sometimes I find myself alone with a hot sausage sandwich smothered in mustard, eyes glued to the television screen; other times the house is packed with my yelling nephews, using breadsticks as swords and dropping dollops of cheese dip on my newly sanded floor. From one day to the next, family mealtimes vary, not just in the time of day, but who's eating and how long you have to prepare the meal.

The best piece of advice I can offer is be prepared, and whatever happens (and it will all go belly-up at times), don't worry about it. Family mealtimes are about wholesome, hearty, and delicious home-cooked dishes that aren't out to impress but to fill hungry bellies. Enjoy cooking the food and take pleasure from your family's enjoyment of what you give them. Don't worry if the pastry cracks or the cheesecake sinks—real, home-cooked food is charming and packed with personality, and you can be sure that it's going to taste fantastic.

Most of the recipes in this book are really easy and pretty quick, too. In fact, most of them, particularly in the "everyday suppers" and "just for two" chapters, go from shopping bag to table in just 30 minutes. All the recipes are easy to follow and packed with shortcuts, and make good use of everyday ingredients, including some good-quality convenience foods, such as refrigerated piecrust dough, curry paste, and pizza dough mix. For those occasions when you do feel like pushing the boat out a little and have a bit more time on your hands, take a look in the "weekends" chapter, which is full of dishes that are stylish enough for entertaining yet still uncomplicated. There are no huge lists of ingredients or time-consuming techniques there, just scrumptious tarts and plenty of slow-cooked meat dishes.

Many of the recipes in this book belie my upbringing in a large Italian family, where daily life was centered around the hustle and bustle of the kitchen. Despite having plenty of other places to go, my siblings and I would jostle for elbow space on the work surface, next to the bubbling pot of rosemary-scented broth. Like most people, I learned to cook from watching my mother and helping with the simpler tasks. What she cooked was classic southern Italian food, which is now incredibly popular everywhere, and it's influence on me is evident throughout this book.

Alongside Mediterranean dishes, including mom's spaghetti with mussels (page 33), you'll also find my best English family dishes, such as crusty-topped shepherd's pie (page 163) and syrup tart, illustrated on the facing page (recipe, page 187). There are also lots of quick favorites that I turn to again and again, like stir-fried steak chile (page 54). Whenever I have great-tasting food in restaurants or cooked for me by friends, I try to recreate the dish at home—silky chicken noodle soup (page 77) and salt-and-pepper spareribs (page 93) are two examples.

There's an old saying in Italy, that "food only tastes good and cakes only rise well if you cook with a happy heart." I hope cooking and eating from this collection of my favorite recipes make your heart as happy as they make mine.

easy family cooking

Preparation is the key to hassle-free family cooking, and the first step is to sort the pantry, fridge, and freezer. Next, assess your equipment, and decide if you need more tools to make your life easier. A little time spent in getting prepared will save you a lot of time later.

Taking stock

Begin by assessing what you have in stock and then having a good clearout. In the pantry, get rid of anything that's out of date and throw out multiples of things you'll never use up, like spices and dried herbs. Be ruthless and discard anything you know you're unlikely to use, however exciting or exotic. That can of guavas may seem wonderful, but is it going to be opened soon or will it linger in the back of the cupboard until it's past its best? If you really can't bear to part with some dried goods that you feel sure will come in handy, give them one week's stay of execution. After that, get rid of them.

The same goes for the freezer. We're all guilty of letting the frost build up next to the ice trays. Now is the time for a clearout. If you must, give the best items one week's grace, but then unplug the freezer, defrost it fully, and clean it. After this you can think about refilling it. The fridge is not usually in such a sorry state, simply because it's used more frequently. But most of us could still do with clearing out some of those neglected opened jars of sauces, relishes, and pastes taking up space on the top shelf.

When you go shopping, think about what you'll need over the next few days. Decide what dishes you're going to cook and plan your shopping list around them. Also, start restocking the foods you want to keep in store. If you have a well-stocked fridge and pantry, and a few standby dishes in the freezer, you'll always be able to feed your family without too much trouble.

The pantry

Keeping a good supply of essential foodstuffs will guarantee that you can rustle up a speedy supper, however basic. While it's true that many products now can be kept for a long time, it's a good idea to try to keep quantities at a realistic minimum in order to avoid wastage—an average-size bag, can, jar, or bottle will do for most families. The only exception to this in my own pantry is canned tomatoes, which I buy by the truckload because I use them so often. If possible, have a rack in a cool cupboard or other cool place for storing sturdy vegetables such as onions and potatoes that don't belong in the fridge. Take them out of any plastic packaging and arrange in the rack so air can circulate around them.

The following is a list of my suggestions for pantry standbys. There are sure to be some foods you wouldn't use and a few missing items that your family wouldn't be without—peanut butter perhaps.

Bottles and jars Sunflower oil, olive oil, extra virgin olive oil, toasted sesame oil, white wine vinegar, soy sauce, chili sauce, Thai fish sauce, curry paste, mayonnaise, tomato ketchup, mustard, honey, wine.

Cans Plum tomatoes, tuna in spring water, anchovies in oil, baked beans, chick peas (garbanzo beans), cannellini beans, red kidney beans, coconut milk and cream, chicken or vegetable broth.

Dried goods Spaghetti or linguine plus pasta shapes (penne, fusilli etc.), noodles, long-grain rice, risotto rice, red lentils, selection of dried herbs and spices, all-purpose flour, baking powder, cornstarch, sea or kosher salt, black peppercorns, granulated sugar, brown sugar, raisins, selection of nuts.

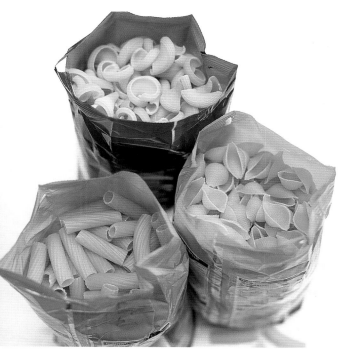

In the chill

Although the pantry needs the most careful planning, the fridge and freezer will need some reorganizing too. Stock the fridge with your daily basics, plus any special ingredients you need for dishes you're planning to cook that week. You'll no doubt build up a collection of opened jars and bottles again, but routinely check them to be sure they are still eatable. Also, carefully look through each shelf and drawer on a regular basis—there's nothing quite as unpleasant as coming across a waterlogged chunk of cucumber. Make sure all food is closely covered, particularly strong-smelling items whose odor could permeate other foods.

The freezer is your savior when it comes to those holidays when you find the fridge is empty by the last night, or rainy days when you can't face a trip to the store. Supermarket freezers are packed with really useful ingredients that you can keep for up to three months, and almost everything else you can buy is labeled to show whether or not it's suitable for the freezer. My freezer is never without a package of pita breads, green peas, lima beans, ground beef, puff pastry, vanilla ice cream, and plenty of ice.

However, without a bit of strict management the freezer will easily reach bursting point within weeks of clearing it out. I find the best solution to this is to divide the space in half, and to use one half for fantastically useful ingredients, such as frozen vegetables and pastry, and the other half for dishes I have cooked myself. Every once in a while, I make a concerted effort to eat every prepared meal in the freezer before freezing any more.

Equipment

Having cleared out and reorganized your stocks of food, you can then move on to assess your kitchen equipment and utensils. Apart from dishes and flatware, you don't usually need multiples of things, and there is a fine line between useful gadgets that make cooking more efficient and other, not so handy items. These are the ones we all have tucked away at the back of the cupboard or drawer or hidden under the stairs gathering dust. Of course, our individual lifestyles play a large part in whether or not these tools will ever be used, so you have to decide on this yourself.

I have an electric juicer that's so worn out I'm too ashamed to have it on the worktop. So I keep it in a cupboard and lug it out each time I need it. Indeed, a good way of knowing whether or not to keep a piece of equipment is to position it on your work surface. If, after a week, it hasn't seen any action at all, then it's off to the charity store with it. Before purchasing any large electrical items, such as a breadmaker or an electric stand mixer, think about it carefully. These appliances are expensive, take up a lot of room, and are only worth having if you are going to use them often.

Here's my recommended "batterie" of basic equipment. The extras, such as juicers and blenders, are up to you. Remember, though, that many items in a basic kit are multi-functional—if you've got a good nonstick frying pan, why give up valuable cupboard space, and hard-earned cash, for a sandwich grill?

Basic kit

A decent set of knives is a must for any cook. Buy good-quality knives that feel comfortable in your grip and make sure you keep them sharp—I recommend you get them professionally sharpened every couple of months. Before too long, even if you're pretty handy with a sharpening steel, your knives won't sharpen and will eventually need properly grinding.

You also need general equipment such as bowls, chopping boards, a colander, a grater, and utensils such as spoons, spatulas, and the like. Where possible, especially with utensils, keep just one or, at a push, two of each. No one truly needs two balloon whisks or several slotted spoons.

I think a full set of pots and pans only needs to consist of three varying sized saucepans with lids— including a really big one for pasta—plus a large nonstick frying pan and a wok or large sauté pan. Buy the best you can afford and treat with care, and your pans will last you for years.

When it comes to pans for baking, always choose nonstick. For cake and tart pans, go for the springform, loose-bottomed variety as they make it much easier to get your cakes and tarts out in one piece. For muffins and individual tarts, look out for ovenproof rubber molds—as they are flexible, the tarts simply pop out. And make sure you buy sturdy roasting pans and baking sheets—inexpensive, thin baking sheets are liable to buckle in the oven.

Electrical items

All electrical kitchen appliances are designed to make your life easier. Although you can manage without them, for example by using a food mill in place of an immersion blender, or a mortar and pestle or heavy knife in place of a mini chopper, most small electrical items are reasonably priced. Although they may have a relatively short life, the time they save is invaluable.

Weighing and measuring If you do any baking, you'll want to have an accurate kitchen scale for weighing ingredients. And every cook needs a set of standard measuring cups and spoons.

Electric mixer A hand-held electric mixer really does save a lot of time as well as tiring wrist-action. I wouldn't fancy making my snowy saffron peaches (page 184) without mine. This appliance is inexpensive and easy to clean.

Immersion blender My hand-held immersion blender is always on the go for smoothing out sauces and soups. It's a lot safer and easier than pouring batches of very hot soup into the goblet of a free-standing electric blender on the worktop.

Small food processor Okay, so you might not use all the fancy blades, but it's fantastic for whizzing up pastry and fine chopping work. If you don't think you'd use it enough, save your cash and instead invest in a mini chopper.

Mini chopper My single most invaluable piece of electrical equipment, this gets used several times a week in my kitchen. It's ideal for chopping small quantities and whizzing up pestos and salsas. A mini chopper is pretty inexpensive, but because the blade is small it does become blunt after extensive use.

Electric juicer This is one of the most used items of equipment in my kitchen. It works by centrifugal force: the high-speed spin separates out the pulp and delivers you delicious, vitamin-packed juice. The most high-tech versions extract the maximum juice possible from the fruit, but they are very expensive. My cheaper version, though stained and a little dented, still works well after five years of vigorous usage.

1 breakfasts

raspberry granola

This is much tastier than any store-bought granola and can be stored in an airtight container for about 2 weeks. I like to serve it with fresh raspberries, but it's also good with other fruit such as sliced banana or moist dried apricots.
Illustrated left

SERVES 12

2 cups old-fashioned rolled oats

1 cup unsweetened dried shredded coconut

1¼ cups roughly chopped pecans

½ teaspoon ground cinnamon

1 tablespoon sunflower oil

6 tablespoons butter, melted

⅓ cup packed light brown sugar

3 tablespoons maple syrup

FOR SERVING:

lowfat milk or plain yogurt

raspberries or other fruit

1 Preheat the oven to 325°F. Mix all the ingredients together and spread out on a large, shallow baking pan, leaving some of the mixture in clumps. Bake for 30–35 minutes until golden and crunchy.

2 Remove the granola from the oven and let cool, then break up into clumps. Serve in bowls with milk or yogurt and fresh raspberries.

fruity muesli yogurt

You need to remember to put this together before you go to bed if you plan to eat it for breakfast the next day, but it takes only a few minutes to prepare. During the hours in the fridge the muesli softens in the yogurt. I love to use pineapple, but you can try it with pretty well any fruit. The granola (above) makes a good alternative to the muesli.

SERVES 4

6 tablespoons Swiss-style muesli

2 fresh pineapple rings, drained and
  roughly chopped

1¼ cups apricot yogurt

¼ cup milk

1 Spoon the muesli into four small bowls or large ramekins. Sprinkle with the chopped pineapple. Mix the yogurt with the milk, then spoon over the fruit. Cover the bowls with plastic wrap and chill in the refrigerator overnight.

2 The next morning, stir the muesli yogurt well and serve.

banana, apricot, and orange blitz

Get the day off to the right start with a glass of this gorgeous tipple.
Illustrated right

SERVES 2
2 bananas
8 moist dried apricots, roughly chopped

1 1/4 –1 3/4 cups freshly squeezed orange juice

1 Peel the bananas, break into pieces, and put in a blender. Add the apricots and a splash of the orange juice, and blend until smooth. Add the remaining juice and blend again until thick and frothy. Pour into glasses and drink right away.

strawberry booster

Don't be put off by the name—believe me, this is delicious and it will certainly send you off to work with a spring in your step.
Illustrated far right

SERVES 1
1/2 cup halved strawberries
1–2 tablespoons thin honey

1 tablespoon wheat germ
1/2 cup milk

1 Place the strawberries, honey, wheat germ, and a splash of milk in a blender and blend until smooth. Add the remaining milk and blend until thick and frothy. Pour into a glass and drink.

mango lassi

A classic Indian lassi is simply yogurt, water, and either sugar or salt, to taste. This one is bolstered with fresh mango and apple cider, and makes a refreshing start to the day.

SERVES 2
1 large, ripe mango, peeled, seeded, and diced
2/3 cup plain yogurt
2/3 cup freshly pressed apple cider

1 Place the mango in a food processor or blender and blend to a smooth purée. Add the yogurt and apple cider, and blend again until smooth and frothy. Pour into ice-filled glasses and serve.

cinnamon crêpes

Hot crêpes straight from the pan with some sliced banana and a drizzle of honey make a fantastic breakfast. These are thin crêpes, so a little batter goes quite a long way: if you have any crêpes left over, layer them up with wax paper in between and freeze.

SERVES 4–6

3/4 cup plus 2 tablespoons all-purpose flour

2 teaspoons ground cinnamon

pinch of salt

1 egg

1 1/4 cups milk

sunflower oil, for frying

FOR SERVING:

4 large bananas

thin honey or maple syrup

1 Sift the flour, cinnamon, and salt into a large bowl. Make a well in the center and add the egg. Using a balloon whisk, gradually beat in the milk to make a smooth batter. If you have time, let it rest in the fridge for 30 minutes.

2 Heat an 8-inch crêpe pan or nonstick frying pan. Add a few drops of oil and, when hot but not smoking, ladle in some batter. Quickly swirl to cover the bottom of the pan thinly. Cook for a minute or so on each side, then slide onto a plate. Repeat with the remaining batter to make at least 12 crêpes.

3 If you want to cook a few crêpes before starting to serve them, stack them up with a square of wax paper between each one.

4 Serve the crêpes as soon as you can: Peel and slice the bananas. Place the crêpes on warm plates, fold them over, and top with the sliced bananas. Drizzle with honey or maple syrup and serve.

breakfast breads

For thousands of years, bread has been a staple food and its wonderful versatility has made it the base, or companion, for most of our meals. And whether it's first thing in the morning or last thing at night, bread is one of the first things we reach for when we need food in a hurry. After all, what can be more instantly satisfying than hot buttered toast and homemade jam?

Over the past few years, the variety of breads in our supermarkets has increased dramatically, with a choice of Italian breads such as ciabatta and focaccia, flatbreads from the Middle East such as pita, rustic French breads, and bagels, now available alongside traditional loaves. And as the range increases, the shelf life of many breads is also extending. Many special purpose breads, such as naan and flour tortillas, are vacuum-packed and last for weeks, and all bread freezes brilliantly. Try the following original breakfast ideas; each serves 4.

▲ **vanilla French toast**
Lightly whisk 4 eggs with 4 tbsp heavy cream in a shallow dish. Dip 8 slices of day-old white bread into the mixture and turn to coat. Heat 2 tbsp sunflower oil in a large frying pan and fry the slices, two or three at a time, for 2–3 minutes on each side until golden. Remove and keep warm while you cook the rest. Sprinkle each slice of French toast with vanilla-flavored sugar, and serve with sliced peaches or other fresh fruit and a spoonful of plain yogurt.

sausage, onion, and mustard biscuits

Cook 8 fresh pork sausages on a hot grill pan, turning, until browned and cooked through; remove and keep warm. Fry 1 sliced large onion in the grill pan for 4 minutes, sprinkling with a little salt and olive oil. Split 4 baking powder biscuits in half. Halve the sausages and put into the biscuits with the onion, a little mustard, and some seasoning; press well to close. Toast on the grill pan for 2–3 minutes each side.

breakfast salad

Broil or fry 8 slices of bacon until golden and crisp; break into pieces. Tear ½ ciabatta loaf into bite-sized pieces and fry in 2 tbsp olive oil for 3–4 minutes until crisp and golden; drain on paper towels. Divide the bacon, ciabatta croûtons, and some arugula leaves among four plates. Poach 4 eggs in simmering water for 4–5 minutes; remove and place on the salad. Whisk 3 tbsp olive oil with 1 tbsp balsamic vinegar and seasoning. Drizzle over the salad and serve.

▲ mozzarella and tomato bagel melt

Preheat the oven to 375°F. Split 4 plain bagels in half horizontally. Arrange sliced mozzarella and sliced ripe tomatoes on the bases. Scatter a few basil leaves on top, drizzle with a little olive oil, and season with salt and pepper. Press the other halves of the bagels on top to make sandwiches. Arrange on a baking sheet and bake for 15–20 minutes until the cheese has melted and the bagels are crisp and golden.

chorizo omelet

Chorizo is fantastic in an omelet—for this I always buy it sliced in a package. Keep the omelet nice and light: don't be tempted to beat the eggs with milk rather than water.

SERVES 1

8 smoked chorizo sausage slices, each roughly torn in half
1 garlic clove, peeled and thinly sliced
2 eggs

1 tablespoon very roughly chopped flat-leaf parsley
sea salt and freshly ground black pepper
hot pepper sauce for serving

1 Heat a large nonstick frying pan. Add the chorizo slices and cook for 2 minutes, then toss in the garlic slices.

2 Meanwhile, break the eggs into a bowl. Using a fork, whisk with 2 tablespoons of water and plenty of seasoning, then stir in the chopped parsley.

3 Pour the egg mixture into the pan and cook over a high heat for a couple of minutes, tilting the pan to swirl the egg, until golden and set. Flip over and cook the other side for 1 minute. Slide onto a warm plate and serve, with some pepper sauce for shaking over and with hot buttered toast.

Parmesan-baked eggs and mushrooms

Because the cream runs and the cheese melts, I recommend you bake these in individual dishes. Serve with hot buttered toast.

SERVES 4

4 tablespoons butter, at room temperature
2 garlic cloves, peeled and crushed
2 tablespoons chopped chives or flat-leaf parsley
4 portobello mushrooms

4 medium eggs
6–8 tablespoons heavy cream
4 tablespoons freshly grated Parmesan cheese
sea salt and freshly ground black pepper

1 Preheat the oven to 350°F. Mix together the butter, garlic, and chives. Cut the stem out of each mushroom and place the caps, gill-side up, in individual heatproof dishes. Season with salt and pepper, and dot with the herb butter. Bake for 15 minutes until softened.

2 Carefully break an egg into each mushroom cap. Swirl a tablespoon or two of cream over each egg and season with salt and pepper, then sprinkle with grated Parmesan. Bake for 6–8 minutes until the egg is just set, then serve.

pancetta potato cakes

These Italian-influenced hash browns are perfect as an on-the-way-out-of-the-door bite. If you have a little more time, top with a poached egg for a scrumptious weekend brunch.

SERVES 4

4 medium russet or all-purpose potatoes,
*   about 1 3/4 lb in total, scrubbed*
4 oz pancetta (Italian bacon) or slab bacon,
*   cubed*
1 shallot, peeled and minced
1 tablespoon vegetable oil (if needed)
sea salt and freshly ground black pepper

1   Cook the whole potatoes in a pan of boiling salted water for 15 minutes.

2   Meanwhile, heat a large nonstick frying pan and add the pancetta. Cook for 3–4 minutes, then add the shallot and cook for a few minutes longer until it has softened and the pancetta is crisp and golden. Using a slotted spoon, transfer the pancetta and shallot to a large bowl.

3   Drain the potatoes. When they are cool enough to handle, coarsely grate them into the bowl. Add some salt and pepper, and mix well together. Firmly shape the mixture in the palm of the hands into eight small ovals.

4   Using the same pan, fry the potato cakes for 3–4 minutes on each side until crisp and golden brown. (There should be enough fat left in the pan from the pancetta, but if not add a splash of oil.)

5   Drain the crisp potato cakes on paper towels and serve while still hot.

Italian fried eggs

A fried egg is a very personal thing. For me, the key is a good crisp base, but feel free to cook yours the way you like it.

SERVES 1

1 plum tomato, thickly sliced
1 thick slice of ciabatta or other rustic bread
2 tablespoons olive oil
1 egg
1 small garlic clove, peeled and thinly sliced
½ hot red chili pepper, thinly sliced (optional)
large handful of snipped chives
½ teaspoon balsamic vinegar
sea salt and freshly ground black pepper

1   Heat a ridged cast-iron grill pan. Lightly brush the tomato slices and bread with a little olive oil. Cook the tomato slices first, for at least 5 minutes. When they're nearly ready, toast the bread in the same pan until nicely char-marked.

2   In the meantime, pour a little olive oil into a small nonstick frying pan and break in the egg. After a minute or so add the garlic, and chili, if using. Cook for a couple of minutes longer, spooning the hot oil over the egg until it is cooked to your liking.

3   Place the grilled bread on a plate and quickly spoon the tomatoes on top.

4   Throw the chives into the egg pan and splash in the balsamic vinegar. Season generously, then slide the egg onto the tomatoes and drizzle the pan juices over the top. Serve right away.

kipper and boiled egg hash

This is a spin on that all-time brilliant Anglo-Indian breakfast dish, kedgeree. I use boil-in-the-bag kippers for it, which I hope you will be able to find in your supermarket too. They are so easy to prepare. I always add the buttery juices from inside the bag to the hash.
Illustrated on previous page

SERVES 4

8-oz package boil-in-the-bag kippers (kippered
  herrings)
6 eggs
2 large red-skinned potatoes, about 1 lb in total,
  peeled and grated
2 tablespoons olive oil
1 garlic clove, peeled and minced
1 tablespoon cumin seeds, roughly crushed
1 teaspoon dried chili flakes
1 bunch of green onions, trimmed and sliced
small bunch of cilantro, roughly chopped
sea salt and freshly ground black pepper
lemon or lime wedges for serving

1 Put the bag of kippers and the eggs into a pan of boiling water and cook for 8 minutes.

2 Meanwhile, thoroughly rinse the grated potatoes and squeeze out as much liquid as possible. Heat the olive oil in a large frying pan and add the potatoes. Season with salt and pepper, and cook for 10–12 minutes over a low heat, stirring occasionally. Add the garlic, cumin, and chili flakes, and cook for a further 1 minute.

3 Drain the kippers and eggs. Cool the eggs under cold running water, then peel and roughly chop them. Open the kipper bag and carefully pour the juices into the potatoes in the frying pan.

4 Roughly flake the kipper flesh with a fork and add to the pan, along with the eggs and green onions. Mix well and heat through gently for 2–3 minutes. Stir in the chopped cilantro and serve, with lemon or lime wedges.

ham and cheese puffs

These are best eaten hot, straight from the oven, but if you have a sandwich grill or toaster with wide slots, you can use that to reheat them. Alternatively, wrap in wax paper and pop into your lunchbox to enjoy cold.

MAKES 4

17½-oz package frozen puff pastry sheets,
  thawed
1 tablespoon Dijon mustard
8 oz Gruyère, Emmental, or Jarslberg
  cheese, thinly sliced
2 oz wafer-thin sliced cooked ham, roughly torn
2 tablespoons butter, melted

1 Preheat the oven to 400°F. Roll out the puff pastry and trim to a 12- by 20-inch rectangle. Cut into eight 6- by 5-inch rectangles.

2 Spread four of the rectangles with the mustard, then cover with the cheese, taking the slices right up to the edges. Scatter the ham over. Place the other four rectangles of puff pastry on top and press down firmly. Squeeze the edges of each puff together between the thumb and forefinger to seal.

3 Arrange the puffs on a baking sheet lined with a silicone baking mat or parchment paper, and brush them with melted butter. Bake for 20 minutes until dark golden. The cheese will ooze out around the edges, but don't worry.

4 Lift the puffs off the mat or paper and let cool slightly for a few minutes before serving. Alternatively, let cool completely and reheat in a sandwich grill or toaster.

2 everyday suppers

spaghetti with mussels

Every time I make this dish—and as anyone who knows me will tell you, that's incredibly often —I'm amazed how quick, simple, and tasty it is. In fact, it is so quick, it's always ready before the table is even set!

SERVES 4

2 ½ lb fresh mussels
11 oz spaghetti
⅔ cup dry white wine
2 garlic cloves, peeled and minced
1 hot red chili pepper, seeded and minced
2 tablespoons chopped parsley
sea salt and freshly ground black pepper
olive oil, for serving

1   Discard any broken mussels, and those that do not close when sharply tapped. Scrub the mussels thoroughly in cold water and pull out any little "beards."

2   Cook the spaghetti in a large pan of boiling salted water according to the package directions until *al dente* (tender, but firm to the bite).

3   Meanwhile, combine the white wine, garlic, chili, and some pepper in a large pan. Bring to a boil and simmer rapidly for 5 minutes. Add the mussels to the pan, cover tightly, and cook for 5 minutes, shaking the pan from time to time, until all the shells have opened (discard any that don't).

4   Drain the pasta and return to the pan. Add the parsley and the mussel mixture, and toss well together. Divide among four warm bowls and drizzle a splash of olive oil over each serving.

butter-roasted cod with green-onion mash

The tricky thing about cooking skinless fish is preventing it from flaking apart as you serve it. Cooking it this way, on sheets of parchment paper, means you can slide the fish onto the plate without it breaking. The soft green-onion mash makes a perfect partner.

SERVES 6

4¹/₂lb russet or all-purpose potatoes, peeled and cubed

6 skinless cod fillet pieces, each about 5 oz

2 tablespoons butter, plus extra for greasing

grated zest and juice of 1 lime

2 bunches of green onions, trimmed and thinly sliced

4–5 tablespoons olive oil

sea salt and freshly ground black pepper

1   Preheat the oven to 425°F. Cook the potatoes in a large pan of boiling salted water for 15–20 minutes until tender.

2   Meanwhile, cut out 6 rectangles of parchment paper just large enough to sit a piece of fish on. Lightly butter each piece of paper and place on a large baking sheet. Put the fish on the paper and dot with the butter. Sprinkle the lime zest over the fish and season with salt and pepper.

3   When the potatoes are almost cooked, put the fish into the oven and roast for 6–8 minutes, depending on thickness, until just cooked.

4   Drain the potatoes well and return to the pan. Mash roughly with a fork, then stir in the lime juice, green onions, and olive oil. Season to taste.

5   Divide the flavored mash among warm serving plates. Gently ease each piece of fish off the paper and slide on top of the mash. Serve immediately.

special fish curry

Though very easy, this is a really stylish supper dish—certainly smart enough to serve for a midweek dinner party. The coconut, limes, and ginger will tickle tastebuds you never knew you had! Serve with basmati or jasmine rice and poppadoms.

Illustrated on previous page

SERVES 6

1 tablespoon sunflower oil
1 large onion, peeled and minced
2 garlic cloves, peeled and minced
2-inch piece of fresh ginger, peeled
  and minced
2 tablespoons hot curry paste
1¼ cups chicken stock
1¾ cups canned coconut milk
2 teaspoons sugar
¼ teaspoon salt
1¾ lb skinless white fish fillet, such as
  pollock, haddock, cod, or monkfish, cut
  into large chunks
1 lb peeled raw tiger shrimp, thawed
  if frozen
juice of 2 limes, or to taste
small handful of cilantro leaves

1 Heat the oil in a large sauté pan and cook the onion, garlic, and ginger for 5 minutes until softened. Stir in the curry paste and cook for 2 minutes. Add the chicken stock and coconut milk, and bring to a gentle simmer (do not boil as the coconut milk could separate).

2 Stir in the sugar and salt, then add the fish. Simmer for just 2 minutes or so until the fish is opaque, then add the shrimp and cook for 1–2 minutes until pink.

3 Add lime juice to taste, then ladle the curry into warm bowls. Scatter the cilantro over and serve.

haddock and cilantro fish cakes

I think this dish offers the best of West and East—our warm, fluffy potato and moist, flaky haddock with the red curry kick and fragrant cilantro of Thailand.

SERVES 4

$2^{1}/_{2}$ lb russet or all-purpose potatoes, peeled
 and diced
1 lb haddock fillet
$1^{1}/_{4}$ cups milk
1 tablespoon Thai red curry paste
1 bunch of green onions, trimmed and
 thinly sliced
$^{1}/_{4}$ cup chopped cilantro
$^{1}/_{4}$ cup all-purpose flour, seasoned
1 egg, beaten
$^{3}/_{4}$ cup dry bread crumbs
2–3 tablespoons sunflower oil
sea salt and freshly ground black pepper
2 limes, cut into wedges, for serving

1   Cook the potatoes in a large pan of boiling water for 15 minutes or so until tender.

2   Meanwhile, place the fish in a large sauté pan and pour the milk over. Cover and bring to a boil, then immediately remove from the heat and let the fish cook in the residual heat for 5 minutes, or until it can be flaked.

3   Drain the potatoes well and return to the pan. Mash until smooth, then stir in the curry paste, green onions, and chopped cilantro.

4   Drain the fish well. Flake roughly, discarding any skin and bones, then lightly stir into the potato mixture. Season with salt and pepper to taste. Shape the mixture into eight cakes, patting to compact them. If you have time, cover and chill so the cakes firm up.

5   Dust the fish cakes in the seasoned flour, then carefully dip them in the beaten egg and then into the bread crumbs to coat on all sides. Heat the oil in a heavy-based frying pan and shallow-fry the fish cakes in batches for 2 minutes on each side until crisp and golden. Drain on paper towels and serve, with lime wedges.

broiled mackerel with lemon-mint drizzle

Mackerel is a wonderful fish—it's packed with all the right kinds of oils and is really economical too. These fillets are cooked under the broiler and are ready in just a few minutes. Serve with a simple leafy salad and some boiled new potatoes for a satisfying, healthy family meal.

SERVES 4

4 whole mackerel, each 11–12 oz, filleted
1 small garlic clove, peeled and quartered
3 green onions, trimmed and roughly
  chopped
1/2 cup mint leaves
1 small lemon
1 tablespoon capers, drained and rinsed
4 tablespoons extra virgin olive oil
sea salt and freshly ground black pepper

1   Preheat the broiler. Season the mackerel fillets, then arrange skin-side up on a foil-lined broiler pan. Cook under the broiler, about 4 inches from the heat, for 3 minutes on each side.

2   Meanwhile, put the garlic and green onions in a small food processor and blend until finely chopped. Tear in the mint leaves, grate in the lemon zest, and add the capers and a little salt. Blend again. Squeeze in the juice from half the lemon and pour in the olive oil, then give one final blitz to blend thoroughly.

3   Place the broiled mackerel on warm serving plates and drizzle the dressing over. Serve immediately.

spiced chicken with herb couscous

I went to Egypt on vacation recently and ate a version of this at a local restaurant two or three times. I loved the crispy, succulent chicken. It's so easy to make, I now do it at home too!

SERVES 4

4 chicken breast halves, each about 4 oz
2–3 teaspoons harissa or other thick chili paste
1¾ cups couscous
1 red onion, peeled and minced
1½ cups hot chicken stock
grated zest and juice of 1 lemon

2 ripe tomatoes, roughly chopped
7 oz feta cheese, crumbled into small pieces
⅓ cup roughly chopped parsley
⅓ cup roughly chopped cilantro
3 tablespoons olive oil
sea salt and freshly ground black pepper
1 lime, cut into wedges, for serving

1   Preheat the broiler. Deeply slash the skin side of the chicken, then rub the harissa into each breast, making sure it goes into the slashes.

2   Arrange the chicken skin-side down on a foil-lined broiler pan. Cook under the broiler, 6–8 inches from the heat, for 6–7 minutes on each side or until cooked through with a crisp skin.

3   Meanwhile, place the couscous and red onion in a large heatproof bowl and pour the hot stock and the lemon juice over. Let soak for 10 minutes until all the liquid has been absorbed.

4   Break up the couscous with a fork, then stir through the tomatoes, feta, lemon zest, herbs, and olive oil. Add salt and pepper to taste.

5   Place the chicken and warm couscous on warm plates and add a lime wedge on the side.

chicken vindaloo

Vindaloo is traditionally associated with Goa, but its origins are actually in Portugal, with the "vin" part of the name meaning wine. It is classically made with pork and always with a wet curry paste. This simplified version uses chicken thighs and a jar of vindaloo curry paste. Serve with basmati rice and some simply cooked leafy greens.

SERVES 4

8 skinless, boneless chicken thighs, about
  2 lb in total, cubed
3 tablespoons vindaloo curry paste
1–2 tablespoons sunflower oil
1 onion, peeled and chopped
4-inch piece of fresh ginger, peeled
  and chopped
2/3 cup dry white wine
1¼ cups hot chicken stock
1 teaspoon dark brown sugar
sea salt and freshly ground black pepper
1 mild green chili pepper, thinly sliced,
  for garnish

1 Place the chicken cubes in a bowl, add the curry paste, and turn to coat. Let marinate in the fridge for at least 30 minutes, or up to 8 hours.

2 Heat the oil in a large pan and cook the chicken for 3–4 minutes. Add the onion and ginger, and cook for a further 5 minutes until golden.

3 Pour in the wine and bubble rapidly for 5 minutes until it evaporates, then stir in the stock and brown sugar. Bring to a boil and simmer gently for 20 minutes. Season with salt and pepper to taste.

4 Divide the curry among warm plates, garnish with the sliced chili, and serve.

lamb and red onion pilaf

The sweetness of red onions and lamb is even more delicious when matched with the savory flavors of cumin and coriander (both spice and herb). The chili kick is warm rather than hot, so this pilaf is fine for all ages. Serve with a leafy salad.

SERVES 4

2–3 tablespoons sunflower oil

2 tablespoons all-purpose flour

1 teaspoon ground cumin

1/2 teaspoon ground coriander

1 teaspoon hot chili powder

1 3/4 lb boneless lamb, cubed

2 red onions, peeled and thickly sliced

2 garlic cloves, peeled and thinly sliced

1 hot red chili pepper, seeded and minced

2 1/4 cups basmati rice

3 cups hot vegetable stock

1 tablespoon hot curry paste

juice of 1 lemon

sea salt and freshly ground black pepper

1/2 cup cilantro leaves, for garnish

1   Pour 2 tablespoons of the oil into a large, heavy casserole and set it over a medium heat. Meanwhile, stir together the flour, cumin, coriander, chili powder, and some salt and pepper.

2   Toss the lamb cubes in the flour mixture, then fry in the hot oil for 5 minutes until nicely browned (you may have to do this in two batches). Remove the lamb with a slotted spoon and set aside.

3   If the pan is dry, add another tablespoon of oil, then cook the onions for 5 minutes. Stir in the garlic and fresh chili and cook for 1 minute longer.

4   Stir in the rice and return the lamb to the casserole, then pour in the stock. Mix in the curry paste, using a wooden spoon to scrape up all the tasty bits from the bottom of the pot, and bring to a boil. Reduce the heat, cover, and simmer gently for 15 minutes until the rice is tender and all the liquid has been absorbed.

5   Stir in the lemon juice and check the seasoning. Divide among warm plates and scatter a few cilantro leaves over each serving.

spiced lamb koftas with tzatziki

This is a classic Greek-style kebab, served in traditional style with tzatziki, pita bread. and salad. It will be on the table in the time it would take to wait for your order in a local Greek taverna.
Illustrated on previous page

SERVES 4

1¼ lb lean ground lamb
1 small onion, peeled and minced
3 tablespoons chopped mint
1 tablespoon chopped oregano
1 teaspoon ground coriander
½ small hothouse cucumber
⅔ cup plain yogurt
1 garlic clove, peeled and crushed
1 lemon, cut into 6 wedges
sea salt and freshly ground black pepper
FOR SERVING:
4 pita breads
salad leaves, such as baby spinach or arugula
small mint leaves

1 Soak 12 wooden skewers in hot water for 10 minutes. Preheat the broiler. Mix together the lamb, onion, 2 tablespoons of the mint, the oregano, coriander, and a seasoning of salt and pepper.

2 Divide the mixture into 12 portions and squeeze around the pre-soaked skewers. Broil the lamb kebabs, about 4 inches from the heat, for 8–10 minutes, turning occasionally, until well browned and cooked through.

3 Meanwhile, grate the cucumber and squeeze out the excess liquid with your hands. Mix with the yogurt, garlic, and remaining mint. Add some salt and squeeze in the juice from one or two of the lemon wedges.

4 Warm the pita breads under the broiler, turning once. Serve the lamb kebabs in the warm pitas, with the salad leaves, tzatziki, and mint leaves. Accompany with the remaining lemon wedges.

grilled lamb leg steaks with summer salad

I can't tell you how many times I've made this, but on warm, summer evenings, when the aromas of rosemary and mint start filling the garden, it's the first choice for the grill. Serve with warmed pita breads or flour tortillas.

SERVES 6

3 tablespoons all-purpose flour
1 tablespoon dried oregano
1 teaspoon dried rosemary
1 teaspoon salt
1 teaspoon steak pepper or coarsely cracked
  black peppercorns
1 teaspoon cayenne
6 lamb leg steaks, bone in, each about 5 oz
1 tablespoon sunflower oil (if using a grill pan)

FOR THE SALAD:

1 hothouse cucumber, peeled and cubed
1 small red onion, peeled and thinly sliced
6 ripe tomatoes
2 tablespoons red wine vinegar
3 tablespoons olive oil
1 cup arugula
1/2 cup mint leaves
sea salt and freshly ground black pepper

1 Mix together the flour, oregano, rosemary, salt, pepper, and cayenne. Lightly dust the lamb leg steaks in the flour mixture. Cook over hot charcoal, or on a lightly oiled, very hot grill pan, for 3–5 minutes on each side until nicely browned but still slightly pink in the center.

2 To make the salad, combine the cucumber and red onion in a large serving bowl. Halve each tomato horizontally, then cut each half into four. Add to the bowl with the vinegar, olive oil, and arugula. Tear in the mint leaves, and season with salt and pepper to taste. Toss gently together.

3 Place the lamb steaks on serving plates. Place the salad and a pile of pita breads or flour tortillas in the center of the table so everyone can help themselves.

Vietnamese beef noodles

This is a modern twist on classic Vietnamese street food, with a clean-flavored, citrusy stock and lots of crunchy vegetables. It's one of my all-time favorite quick suppers.

SERVES 4

1 lb thin Asian egg noodles
4 oz baby corn
7 oz small bok choy
5 cups hot chicken stock
1½-inch piece of fresh ginger, peeled and
   cut into matchsticks
12 oz very thin steaks (minute steaks)

1 tablespoon chili sauce
1 cup snow peas
2–3 tablespoons soy sauce
juice of 2 limes, or to taste
1½ cups bean sprouts
handful of cilantro leaves

1   Cook or soak the noodles in boiling water according to package directions.

2   Halve the baby corn and bok choy lengthwise. Pour the stock into a large pan, add the ginger, and bring to a boil.

3   Meanwhile, heat a nonstick grill or frying pan until very hot. Brush the steaks with the chili sauce, then place on the hot grill pan and cook for 1 minute on each side. Transfer to a plate and set aside to rest for a couple of minutes.

4   Add the baby corn, bok choy, and snow peas to the stock, return to a simmer, and cook for about 2 minutes until just tender. Stir in the soy sauce and lime juice to taste.

5   Drain the noodles and divide among four warm bowls. Add the bean sprouts and ladle the stock on top. Thinly slice the steaks and add to the bowls. Scatter cilantro leaves over and serve.

dill-pickle cheeseburgers

I always seem to end up making these whenever my nephews come to visit. I don't know whether it's the crunchy pickles, or the melting cheese, or the lovely juicy burgers, but the plates always come back clean. If you want to spice up the burgers, whiz 1 or 2 seeded hot red chili peppers with the bread and parsley.

SERVES 6

2 slices of white bread, crusts removed
1/3 cup roughly chopped flat-leaf parsley
1 egg
1 3/4 lb lean ground beef
2 dill pickles, minced, or 2 tablespoons
  minced gherkins
sea salt and freshly ground black pepper

FOR SERVING:

6 hamburger buns
6 slices Port Salut, Jarlsberg, or Cheddar cheese
tomato ketchup (optional)

1   Tear the white bread into pieces and place in a food processor with the parsley. Blend until the bread is broken into crumbs. Transfer to a large bowl.

2   Using a wooden spoon, mix in the egg, beef, pickles, and plenty of salt and pepper. You may need to use your hands to work the mixture together.

3   Preheat a grill pan or the broiler. Shape the mixture into 8 patties just under 1/2 inch thick. Cook on the grill pan, or under the broiler, for 3–4 minutes on each side until nicely browned and cooked to your taste.

4   Split open the buns and place a burger on the bottom of each. Top with a slice of cheese and a squirt of tomato ketchup, if you like, then put on the lid and serve with salad.

stir-fried steak chile

This is a guaranteed winner in my house and it's incredibly quick to make—about 15 minutes from shopping bag to table. My friend Angela adds a shot of espresso coffee to her chile, which imparts a real depth of flavor. If you want to try this trick, add it with the steak sauce.

SERVES 4

1 tablespoon vegetable oil

1¼ lb sirloin steak, cubed

1 bunch of green onions, trimmed and
thickly sliced

4 mild green chili peppers, seeded and roughly
chopped

1 teaspoon cumin seeds

1 teaspoon cayenne or hot chili powder

4 ripe tomatoes, roughly chopped

14 oz canned cannellini beans, drained

1 tablespoon steak sauce

2 tablespoons roughly chopped flat-leaf parsley

sea salt and freshly ground black pepper

FOR SERVING:

²/₃ cup sour cream

²/₃ cup fresh guacamole

tortilla chips

1 Heat a wok, add the oil, and, when it is very hot, add the steak. Stir-fry for 2–3 minutes until starting to brown. Add the onions, chilies, cumin seeds, and cayenne, and stir-fry for 2 minutes.

2 Lower the heat and stir in the tomatoes, then cook over a high heat for a couple of minutes until they begin to soften. Add the cannellini beans and steak sauce, and simmer gently for 5 minutes longer or until piping hot. Season with salt and pepper to taste, and stir in the parsley.

3 Serve the chile with plain boiled rice, the sour cream, guacamole, and tortilla chips.

pan-fried pork chops with rosemary and spinach

When it comes to pork, I always say take it nice and slow. When I've rubbed the chops with oil and seasoning, I cook them really gently until they're beautifully golden but still tender and moist. Serve this with mashed potatoes.

SERVES 4

4 pork chops, each about 6 oz
4 long rosemary sprigs
1 tablespoon olive oil
2¼ lb leaf spinach, washed
1 tablespoon butter
1 garlic clove, peeled and thinly sliced
sea salt and freshly ground black pepper

1   Push a metal skewer horizontally through each chop and remove, then push the rosemary sprig through each hole. Rub the chops with olive oil and season with salt and pepper.

2   Preheat a nonstick frying pan and gently cook the chops for 15–20 minutes until nicely browned and cooked through.

3   Meanwhile, cram the spinach into a large pan, cover with a tight-fitting lid, and cook gently for 5 minutes until wilted. Tip into a colander and press with a wooden spoon to extract the excess water.

4   Transfer the pork chops to a warm plate and set aside in a warm spot to rest for 5 minutes.

5   Add the butter to the hot frying pan, then toss in the garlic and cook for a minute or so. Add the wilted spinach and some seasoning, and cook gently for 4–5 minutes, stirring from time to time.

6   Serve the chops with the soft spinach, and with any juices from the pork spooned over.

fusilli with Savoy cabbage and crispy bacon

Definitely delicious, this one's a real winner when you're feeling a bit strapped for cash. I like to eat it from a bowl in front of the television when the rain is pouring down outside.

SERVES 4

1¼ lb fusilli or other pasta shapes
½ head Savoy cabbage, shredded
6 bacon slices
2 tablespoons olive oil
1 onion, peeled and minced
2 garlic cloves, peeled and thinly sliced
2 hot red chili peppers, halved, seeded, and
  thinly sliced
6 tablespoons freshly grated Parmesan cheese
sea salt and freshly ground black pepper

1   Cook the pasta in a large pan of boiling salted water according to the package directions until *al dente* (tender, but firm to the bite). About 5 minutes before the pasta is due to finish cooking, add the cabbage to the pan.

2   Meanwhile, cut the bacon slices across into ½-inch strips. Heat the olive oil in a frying pan and cook the bacon for 1–2 minutes. Add the onion, garlic, and chilies, and cook for 5 minutes longer until the onion has softened.

3   Drain the pasta and cabbage well and return to the pan. Season the bacon mixture with a little salt and plenty of pepper, then stir into the pasta and cabbage. Sprinkle in the Parmesan and toss together. Divide among warm bowls and serve immediately, with more grated Parmesan.

sausage piece penne

This is a really satisfying, sustaining dish. To turn it into a warming winter casserole, transfer to a baking dish, sprinkle with freshly grated Parmesan cheese, and bake at 400°F for 30 minutes until the top is crusty and golden brown.

SERVES 6

2 lb large, fresh pork sausages
2 onions, peeled and chopped
4 garlic cloves, peeled and chopped
2 hot red chili peppers, seeded and minced
3 sage sprigs
28 oz canned crushed tomatoes
1 teaspoon brown sugar
1¼ lb penne or other pasta shapes
sea salt and freshly ground black pepper
freshly grated Parmesan cheese, for serving

1 Cut the sausages into 1-inch pieces. Heat a large sauté pan or heavy casserole and cook the sausage pieces for 5 minutes until lightly browned.

2 Drain off the excess fat to leave just a thin coating in the pan, then add the onions and garlic. Cook for 10 minutes, stirring occasionally, until golden brown.

3 Stir in the chilies and sage, and cook for 1 minute. Add the tomatoes with their juice, the sugar, and some salt and pepper. Bring to a boil, then partially cover and simmer gently for 40 minutes until dark and a little pulpy.

4 Meanwhile, cook the pasta in a large pan of boiling salted water according to the package directions until *al dente* (tender, but firm to the bite). Drain well and return to the pan, then add the sausage sauce and toss to mix.

5 Divide the hot pasta among warm bowls. Serve with Parmesan, and don't forget the pepper mill.

chorizo and cannellini bean soup

Chorizo sausage has a wonderful smoky flavor, which gives this hearty soup a real taste of Spain. It's important to use a dry, mealy-textured potato here so it can almost dissolve into the soup and give a lovely thick finish. Serve with warm crusty bread.

SERVES 4

2 tablespoons olive oil

2 garlic cloves, peeled and chopped

1 onion, peeled and chopped

1¼ lb russet or all-purpose potatoes, peeled
   and diced

2 teaspoons smoked paprika

4 cups hot vegetable stock

9 oz smoked chorizo sausage, roughly diced

14 oz canned cannellini beans, drained

sea salt and freshly ground black pepper

2 tablespoons chopped parsley, for garnish

1   Heat the olive oil in a large saucepan. Add the garlic, onion, and potatoes, and cook gently for about 10 minutes until golden. Stir in the paprika and stock, and bring to a boil. Lower the heat and simmer for 15 minutes.

2   Stir in the chorizo sausage and cannellini beans, and cook for 5 minutes or so until piping hot. Season with a little salt and plenty of black pepper, then ladle into warm bowls and serve sprinkled with the chopped parsley.

pantry suppers

We all have moments when the fridge is empty and we just can't face going to the supermarket, or friends turn up just as we are about to start cooking supper. These are the times when we turn to the pantry for help. Let's face it: a well-stocked pantry is the lazy cook's best friend. (For suggestions of useful items to keep in stock for impromptu meals, see page 9.)

If you always keep the essentials on hand, you'll be safe in the knowledge that you can keep your family fed and watered, even in an emergency. Good starchy carbohydrates—such as rice, pasta, noodles, and bread—form the basis for almost every meal, so make sure you have them in stock. With just a few flavorsome additions and a couple of fresh ingredients, they can be turned into a truly satisfying supper, usually in next to no time. Here are a few quick ideas using pantry standbys. Each serves 2.

▲ lemony lentil and pasta soup
Cook 1 chopped onion and 1 chopped carrot in 1 tbsp olive oil with a little chopped garlic for a few minutes to soften. Stir in 14 oz canned tomatoes with juice, ¼ cup red lentils, and 2 cups vegetable stock. Bring to a boil and simmer for 30 minutes until the lentils are tender. Cook ½ cup fusilli or other pasta shapes in a separate pan of boiling salted water until *al dente*. Once the lentils are cooked, stir in the drained pasta and a good squeeze of lemon juice. Season and serve.

spiced chick pea biriyani

Heat 1 tbsp sunflower oil in a stovetop-to-oven casserole and cook 2 large sliced onions for 10 minutes until golden. Add ½ tsp cumin or mustard seeds and cook for 1 minute. Stir in 1 cup basmati rice, 14 oz canned chick peas, drained, 2 tbsp curry paste, 2 tbsp golden raisins, 2½ cups hot vegetable stock, salt, and pepper. Cover and cook in the oven at 375°F for 25 minutes until the rice is tender. Scatter with salted cashews.

satay noodles

Simmer 4 oz Asian egg noodles in boiling water for 3–4 minutes until tender, then drain. Heat a splash of sunflower oil in a wok and cook 1 sliced large red bell pepper for 2–3 minutes on a high heat. Add the noodles, 1 cup coconut cream, ½ cup roughly chopped salted or dry-roast peanuts, a dash of soy sauce, and a squeeze of lime juice. Heat, stirring, until piping hot. Divide among bowls and scatter some cilantro or sliced green onions on top.

▲ cheesy bean hash

Using a fork, roughly mash 2 lb boiled potatoes with 14 oz canned baked beans and a pinch of dried chili flakes. Heat a little sunflower oil in a large nonstick frying pan. Add the mash and cook over a low heat, without turning, for 15 minutes until the bottom is crisp and golden. Turn the hash over, roughly breaking it up, then let cook for 15 minutes until the base is crisp. Stir through a handful of shredded Cheddar cheese, top with a dollop of sweet chili sauce or ketchup, and serve.

butternut chowder with cheese toasties

Choose an orange-fleshed squash, such as butternut or kabocha, for this recipe as these cook down to a wonderful velvety-textured soup. In common with many other soups, this benefits from a night in the fridge so the flavors can really develop.

SERVES 4

2 tablespoons olive oil

2 onions, peeled and minced

2 garlic cloves, peeled and roughly chopped

8 cups peeled and cubed butternut or
   kabocha squash

4 cups hot vegetable stock

4 thyme sprigs

1 cup crème fraîche

sea salt and freshly ground black pepper

FOR THE CHEESE TOASTIES:

3 tablespoons butter, at room temperature

8 slices of white bread

2 cups shredded Gruyère cheese

1/4 cup snipped chives or garlic chives

1 Heat the olive oil in a large saucepan and cook the onions, garlic, and squash over a gentle heat for about 10 minutes until the onion has softened. Pour in the hot stock and stir in the thyme. Cover and simmer for 30 minutes until tender.

2 Meanwhile, butter the bread. Make up four sandwiches with the cheese and chives, keeping the butter on the outside of the sandwiches. Preheat a grill pan or large nonstick frying pan, and cook the sandwiches, two at a time, for 2–3 minutes on each side until golden brown and the cheese is molten inside. Keep hot.

3 Remove the woody thyme stems from the soup, then purée with an immersion blender or in a blender goblet until smooth. Return to the pan if necessary. Stir in the crème fraîche and heat through gently without boiling. Check the seasoning.

4 Cut the toasties into squares or fingers. Ladle the soup into warm bowls and serve with the toasties.

cheese and tomato macaroni

Everyone loves macaroni cheese and this is a fantastic version. It skips the hassle of making a cheese sauce and packs even more flavor with the addition of roasted sweet cherry tomatoes.

SERVES 4

9 oz cherry tomatoes
1 tablespoon olive oil
12 oz macaroni (about 2 cups)

1 cup mascarpone cheese
1 tablespoon Dijon mustard
3 cups shredded fontina cheese
sea salt and freshly ground black pepper

1 Preheat the oven to 425°F. Place the cherry tomatoes in a 2-quart baking dish. Drizzle the olive oil over them and season with salt and pepper. Roast for 15 minutes until the tomatoes have softened slightly and the skins have split.

2 Meanwhile, cook the macaroni in a large pan of boiling salted water according to the package directions until *al dente* (tender, but firm to the bite).

3 In a bowl, combine the mascarpone, mustard, and fontina cheese, stirring until evenly blended.

4 Drain the pasta and return to the pan. Stir in the cheese mixture, then the roasted tomatoes and season with salt and pepper to taste. Tip the mixture back into the baking dish used for the tomatoes. Bake for 25–30 minutes until golden brown and bubbling. Let stand for a few minutes, then serve straight from the dish.

roasted pepper pizzettes

If there's a better time to make these than on a lazy sunny afternoon, then I've yet to find it. The sweet, bursting cherry tomatoes and creamy soft mozzarella will have everyone coming back for more!

SERVES 6

1¼ lb pizza dough mix
flour, for dusting
1 lb yellow cherry tomatoes
10 oz bottled roasted peppers in olive oil,
  drained
11 oz mozzarella cheese, drained
2 tablespoons olive oil
sea salt and freshly ground black pepper
basil leaves, for garnish

1 Preheat the oven to 400°F. Empty the pizza dough mix into a bowl and mix with warm water according to the package directions, to make a soft dough. Knead vigorously on a lightly floured surface for 5 minutes until smooth.

2 Divide the dough into six even-sized balls and roll out each roughly to an 8-inch round. Transfer the rounds to two nonstick baking sheets and let rise for 10 minutes.

3 Meanwhile, halve the cherry tomatoes, cut the roasted peppers into strips, and dice the mozzarella. Arrange on top of the pizzas, drizzle with the olive oil, and season with salt and pepper. Bake for 20 minutes until risen and golden brown. Tear the basil leaves over the pizzettes and serve.

caramelized pepper spaghetti

Bell peppers are often quickly stir-fried, which leaves them wonderfully crunchy, but sometimes it's better to let gentle slow-cooking release their natural sweetness.

SERVES 6

4 tablespoons olive oil

6 bell peppers (3 red and 3 yellow), cored, seeded, and thinly sliced

1 large onion, peeled and thinly sliced

1 1/2 lb spaghetti

2 garlic cloves, peeled and thinly sliced

1 tablespoon balsamic vinegar

1/2 cup basil leaves

1/4 cup freshly grated Parmesan cheese

sea salt and freshly ground black pepper

1 Heat the olive oil in a large sauté pan and very gently cook the peppers and onion with some salt and pepper over a low heat for 40–45 minutes, stirring from time to time, until the peppers become very soft and the onion is dark golden.

2 About 10 minutes before the peppers will be ready, cook the spaghetti in a large pan of boiling salted water according to the package directions until *al dente* (tender, but firm to the bite). Stir the garlic into the peppers and cook for a few more minutes. Add the vinegar and check the seasoning.

3 Drain the pasta well and return to the pan. Tear in the basil, then add the pepper mixture and Parmesan. Toss well, then serve.

garlic mushroom linguine

This easy pasta dish uses the classic pairing of garlic and mushrooms. Serve with a full-bodied Italian red wine and plenty of Parmesan.

SERVES 4

1 lb linguine

4 tablespoons butter

2 tablespoons olive oil

3 garlic cloves, peeled and chopped

1 1/4 lb cremini mushrooms, thickly sliced

juice of 1 lemon, or to taste

1/3 cup chopped tarragon or parsley

sea salt and freshly ground black pepper

freshly grated Parmesan cheese, for serving

1 Cook the pasta in a large pan of boiling salted water according to the package directions until *al dente* (tender, but firm to the bite). Meanwhile, heat the butter and olive oil in a large frying pan and fry the garlic for 1 minute. Add the mushrooms with lemon juice to taste and cook for 10 minutes, stirring only once or twice, until tender and golden brown. Season generously.

2 Drain the pasta well and return to the pan. Add the mushrooms and herbs, toss well, and serve, with Parmesan to hand around.

pea, mascarpone, and mint risotto

This is a lovely soft risotto that's brought to the table with the mascarpone just melting. I like to serve it with chilled white wine or icy cold beers. You can make this with any type of risotto rice, but the elegant carnaroli grain is always my first choice.

SERVES 4

1 tablespoon olive oil

1 large onion, peeled and chopped

2 garlic cloves, peeled and chopped

1³/₄ cups carnaroli or other risotto rice

3 rosemary sprigs

²/₃ cup Italian dry white wine

5 cups hot vegetable stock

2 cups frozen green peas

1 cup mascarpone cheese

¹/₄ cup roughly chopped mint

sea salt and freshly ground black pepper

2 tablespoons freshly grated Parmesan cheese,
   for serving

1   Heat the olive oil in a large, heavy-based saucepan, add the onion and garlic, and cook for about 5 minutes until the onion has softened.

2   Stir in the rice and rosemary, then add the wine and cook vigorously for 2–3 minutes until it has been absorbed. Pour in half of the stock and let cook for 10 minutes or until the stock has been absorbed, stirring from time to time.

3   Add the rest of the stock and continue to cook for a further 5 minutes, then add the peas. Cook for another 5 minutes, stirring occasionally, until all the liquid has been absorbed and the rice is tender. Season with salt and pepper to taste, and remove the woody rosemary stems. Ripple through the mascarpone and mint.

4   Before the mascarpone has completely melted, divide the risotto among warm bowls and top each with a sprinkle of Parmesan and a large grinding of black pepper. Serve swiftly.

3 weekends

Spanish shrimp soup

This is version of a classic bisque. The addition of paprika and paella rice give the soup an inviting Spanish flavor.

SERVES 6

1³/₄ lb raw shrimp (any size will do),
  thawed if frozen
2 tablespoons butter
2 shallots, peeled and sliced
2 garlic cloves, peeled and sliced
2 ripe tomatoes, roughly chopped

1 rosemary sprig
1 tablespoon smoked paprika
pinch of dried chili flakes
²/₃ cup dry white wine
¹/₃ cup short-grain rice, such as paella
  or risotto rice
sea salt and freshly ground black pepper

1   Peel the shrimp and set aside, reserving the shells. Heat the butter in a large pan and cook the shallots and garlic for 2 minutes. Add the shrimp shells and cook for 3–4 minutes longer.

2   Stir in the tomatoes, rosemary, paprika, and chili flakes, and cook for 1 minute. Add the wine and cook vigorously for a couple of minutes, then add 8 cups water. Bring to a boil, then cover and simmer gently for 20 minutes.

3   Strain the stock into a clean pan, then stir in the rice and some salt and pepper. Bring to a gentle boil and simmer for 30 minutes until the rice is very soft.

4   Add the shrimp and cook for 3–5 minutes, depending on the size, until they are pink. Blend until smooth using an immersion blender, or in a blender goblet, and then reheat gently. Ladle into warm bowls and serve with warm crusty bread.

smoked haddock and shrimp pie

Everyone loves this fish pie. There's something about the fluffy, cheesy potatoes, juicy seafood, and creamy chive-speckled sauce that makes it irresistible. It's a perfect winter supper that's easier to make than you think.

SERVES 8

4½ lb russet or all-purpose potatoes, peeled
   and cubed
4 cups milk
1¾ lb smoked haddock fillets (finnan haddie)
7 tablespoons butter
6 tablespoons all-purpose flour

½ cup shredded Cheddar cheese
1¼ cups sour cream
1 cup frozen green peas, thawed
1 lb peeled raw tiger shrimp, thawed
   if frozen
¼ cup snipped chives
sea salt and freshly ground black pepper

1 Cook the potatoes in a large pan of boiling salted water for 15–20 minutes until tender.

2 Meanwhile, pour the milk into a sauté pan and add the smoked haddock. Bring gently to a boil, then remove from the heat and let stand for 5 minutes. Using a slotted spoon, transfer the smoked haddock to a plate and set aside. Measure ¾ cup of the milk for the mash; the rest will be used in the sauce.

3 To make the sauce, melt 6 tablespoons of the butter in a heavy-based pan. Stir in the flour and cook for 1 minute. Gradually whisk in the milk for the sauce. Bring to a boil, stirring, then simmer gently for 3–4 minutes.

4 Preheat the oven to 400°F. Drain the potatoes and mash well. Stir in the milk reserved for the mash along with the remaining butter, the cheese, and some seasoning.

5 Stir the sour cream and peas into the sauce along with the shrimp, and heat gently for a couple of minutes without boiling. Pour into a deep baking dish. Stir in the chives. Flake in the haddock, discarding any skin, and season to taste.

6 Spoon the mash over the top to cover the filling and rough up the surface using a fork. Place the dish on a baking sheet and bake for 30 minutes until bubbling around the edges and golden brown.

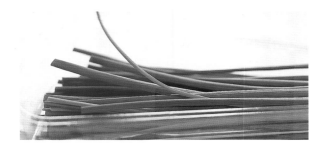

olive oil-poached salmon with linguine and lemon

This is very simple, but quite an elegant dish. Slowly cooking the salmon in olive oil gives it a lovely flavor and keeps it perfectly moist.

SERVES 6

1 3/4 lb salmon fillet, cut into 6 even-sized pieces
1 lemon, peeled and thinly sliced
2 tablespoons roughly chopped tarragon
1 teaspoon black peppercorns, roughly crushed
1 teaspoon salt
1 cup olive oil
1 1/4 lb linguine
1/2 cup minced rehydrated dry-pack sun-dried
  tomatoes
2 handfuls of arugula

1   Preheat the oven to 300°F. Arrange the pieces of salmon in a shallow baking pan and place the lemon slices on top. Scatter the tarragon, peppercorns, and salt over the salmon, and pour on the olive oil. Bake for 30 minutes until the salmon is cooked.

2   Meanwhile, cook the pasta in a large pan of boiling salted water according to the package directions until *al dente* (tender, but firm to the bite). Drain and return to the pan.

3   Lift the salmon out of the oil and break it into large flakes, directly into the pan of pasta. Add 1–2 tablespoons of the olive oil, along with the lemon slices, sun-dried tomatoes, and arugula, and toss together gently. Divide among warm bowls and serve.

silky chicken noodle soup

My friend, chef Ben O'Donoghue, showed me how to cook chicken this way—the bird is steeped in a fragrant stock rather than poached. It is a traditional Chinese method and gives the chicken a wonderful tender texture.

SERVES 8

1 chicken, about 4½ lb, cut into 8 pieces

1 red onion, peeled and roughly chopped

6 garlic cloves, peeled and thickly sliced

1½-inch piece of fresh ginger, peeled and thickly sliced

2 lemon grass stalks, lightly flattened with a rolling pin

2 hot red chili peppers, thickly sliced

8 kaffir lime leaves, fresh or dried

1 teaspoon salt

8 oz fine Chinese egg noodles

8 oz bok choy, sliced

4 oz shiitake mushrooms, sliced

3 tablespoons soy sauce

1 tablespoon wine vinegar

2 cups bean sprouts

handful of cilantro leaves

1 teaspoon toasted sesame oil

1 Remove the skin from the chicken pieces, then place them in a large pot. Add the onion, garlic, ginger, lemon grass, chilies, lime leaves, and salt. Cover with water—you will need about 3 quarts. Bring to a boil, skimming off any surface residue. Cover with a lid, remove from the heat, and let cool. The chicken will cook in the residual heat (once cooled, it can be chilled overnight).

2 Strain the stock into a clean pan. Lift out the chicken from the strainer and discard the flavorings. Using your fingers, tear the chicken meat from the bones and set aside. Gently reheat the stock.

3 Meanwhile, cook the egg noodles in a separate pan of boiling water according to the package directions. Drain the noodles and divide among eight warm bowls.

4 Stir the shredded chicken, bok choy, and mushrooms into the hot stock and cook for 1 minute. Add the soy sauce and vinegar.

5 Pile the bean sprouts on top of the noodles, then ladle in the chicken and vegetable broth. Scatter some cilantro leaves over and add a drop or two of sesame oil to each bowl. Serve at once.

Peking duck noodles

Peking duck does take a bit of preparation time, but my version is much simpler than the classic Chinese method and well worth the effort. It makes an impressive dinner party dish, too.

SERVES 6

1 plump duck, about 4½ lb
1 tablespoon dark brown sugar
2 teaspoons sea salt
1 lb thin Chinese egg noodles
1 tablespoon sunflower oil
1½-inch piece fresh ginger, peeled and diced
1 vegetable bouillon cube

1 tablespoon cornstarch, mixed with a little water
2 tablespoons sweet chili sauce
1 tablespoon soy sauce
4 Napa cabbage leaves, shredded
1 hot red chili pepper, seeded and minced
4 green onions, thinly sliced
small handful of basil leaves, for garnish

1 Pierce the duck in several places with a skewer. Place on a rack over a roasting pan. Pour 4 cups boiling water over the duck. Drain away the water. Pat the duck dry with paper towels, then put back on the rack. Mix the sugar and salt, and rub into the duck skin. Leave in a cool, dry place for 2 hours.

2 Preheat the oven to 400°F. Pat the duck dry again, then roast for 1½ hours, basting from time to time, until the skin is crisp and dark and the meat is cooked through—pierce the thigh to check that it's not at all pink. Let rest for 10 minutes.

3 Meanwhile, cook or soak the noodles in boiling water according to package directions; drain. Heat a wok, add the oil, and, when hot, add the noodles and ginger. Cook for 3 minutes without stirring so the noodles on the base crisp. Dissolve the bouillon cube in 1¼ cups boiling water.

4 Stir to break up the noodles. Add the stock, cornstarch, chili and soy sauces, Napa cabbage, chili pepper, and green onions. Stir-fry for 2–3 minutes. Using a cleaver or strong knife, cut the duck into pieces. Divide the noodle mixture among warm plates and top with the duck. Garnish with the basil.

chunky chicken and potato pie

A wonderful pie, with a delicious creamy flavor. It freezes very well, but make sure you allow plenty of time for it to thaw in the fridge.

SERVES 6

1 tablespoon olive oil

9 large skinless, boneless chicken thighs, trimmed and quartered

2 potatoes, peeled and cut into 3/4-inch dice

1 red onion, peeled and cut into wedges

2 medium leeks, trimmed and thickly sliced

3 garlic cloves, peeled and halved

1 bay leaf

1 tablespoon all-purpose flour

1/3 cup frozen green peas

2/3 cup crème fraîche

2/3 cup chicken stock

small bunch of flat-leaf parsley, roughly chopped

14 oz puff pastry, thawed if frozen

1 egg, beaten, for glazing

sea salt and freshly ground black pepper

1   Preheat the oven to 375°F. Put the olive oil in a small roasting pan or a large baking dish and add the chicken, potatoes, red onion, leeks, garlic cloves, bay leaf, and flour. Toss well together, then season with salt and pepper. Roast for 25–30 minutes until tender, turning the chicken and vegetables occasionally.

2   Add the frozen peas, then stir in the crème fraîche, chicken stock, and parsley. If you have time, let the filling cool.

3   Roll out the pastry to 1 inch larger all around than the size of the roasting pan or baking dish. Lay the pastry over the filling, tucking in the edges down the sides of the pan, or pressing them onto the rim of the dish (first brush the rim with a little water).

4   Brush the top of the pie with beaten egg to glaze, then bake for 25–30 minutes until the pastry is risen and golden. Serve hot.

lemon chicken with sweet potato and rosemary mash

Preserved lemons lend a delicious Middle-Eastern flavor to roast chicken, and soft, creamy roast sweet potato purée is a fabulous accompaniment.

SERVES 6

2 chickens, each about 3¹/₄ lb, each cut into
  8 pieces
12 garlic cloves
8 thyme sprigs
8 small preserved or pickled lemons, halved
2 tablespoons butter
sea salt and freshly ground black pepper

FOR THE MASH:
4¹/₂ lb sweet potatoes, peeled and
  thickly sliced
1 tablespoon olive oil
1 tablespoon chopped rosemary
5–6 tablespoons crème fraîche

1   Preheat the oven to 400°F. Pack the chicken pieces, garlic, thyme, and lemons snugly into a large roasting pan. Season generously with salt and pepper, then dot with the butter. Roast for 40 minutes until golden brown and cooked through.

2   Meanwhile, put the sweet potato slices in another roasting pan and stir in the olive oil, rosemary, and some salt and pepper. Roast for 30 minutes until tender and golden. Roughly mash the sweet potatoes in the pan, then stir in the crème fraîche using a wooden spoon.

3   Divide the chicken among warm plates, making sure everyone gets some garlic and preserved lemon. Serve the sweet potato mash alongside.

lamb and red cabbage hotpot

Here is the perfect comfort food to warm up a cold winter evening. This hearty dinner takes a while to cook but it's very easy to prepare. I've used a boned shoulder of lamb, but you could use leaner boned leg if you prefer.

Illustrated on previous page

SERVES 6

2–3 tablespoons vegetable oil
3¼ lb boned shoulder of lamb, trimmed of
  excess fat and cut into large cubes
2 tablespoons all-purpose flour
1 large onion, peeled and sliced
4 garlic cloves, peeled and thinly sliced
6 thyme sprigs
1 small head red cabbage, about 1¼ lb,
  cored and thinly sliced
⅔ cup ruby port
3 cups lamb stock
4 teaspoons balsamic vinegar
2¼ lb red-skinned potatoes
2 tablespoons butter, melted
sea salt and freshly ground black pepper

1 Heat the oil in a large stovetop-to-oven casserole. Dust the lamb with the flour and fry in batches for 3–4 minutes, stirring, until nicely browned all over.

2 Once all the meat is browned and set aside on a plate, add the onion to the pot and cook for 5–8 minutes until soft and golden. Add the garlic and thyme, and cook for a further minute or so.

3 Return the lamb to the pot, along with any juices on the plate. Stir in the cabbage, port, stock, and vinegar. Bring to a boil, then cover and simmer gently for 1–1½ hours until the lamb is very tender.

4 Meanwhile, preheat the oven to 400°F. Cook the potatoes in boiling salted water for 15 minutes. Drain and thickly slice.

5 Uncover the casserole and arrange the sliced potatoes over the lamb and and cabbage. Brush the potatoes with the melted butter and place in the oven. Bake, uncovered, for 30 minutes until they are golden brown. Serve straight from the casserole.

slow-roast leg of lamb in wine

Slow-cooking a whole leg of lamb in wine ensures it turns out meltingly tender and juicy. Rosemary, the classic herb for lamb, adds flavor and fragrance, and is balanced by a touch of sweetness from red-currant jelly.

SERVES 6

2 tablespoons olive oil
1 leg of lamb, about 4¹/₂ lb
2 tablespoons all-purpose flour
2 onions, peeled and thinly sliced
4 rosemary sprigs
4 garlic cloves, peeled and thinly sliced
2 bottles dry white wine, or 1 bottle plus
  3 cups lamb stock
2 tablespoons red-currant jelly
sea salt and freshly ground black pepper

1 Preheat the oven to 325°F. Pour the olive oil into a large, heavy roasting pan and set it on the stovetop to heat. Season the lamb, then roll it in the flour. Brown the lamb all over in the hot oil for 5–10 minutes.

2 Add the onions and cook for 5–10 minutes longer, turning the lamb and stirring the onions, until both are nicely browned. Add the rosemary, garlic, white wine (plus stock if using), and red-currant jelly. Bring to a simmer.

3 Transfer to the oven and cook for 3–3¹/₂ hours, basting the lamb now and again with the liquid. There should be a good quantity of liquid left in the bottom of the pan to serve with the lamb; if you feel it is getting too dry, just cover with foil.

4 Take the lamb out of the pan, place on a large warm platter, and set aside to rest in a warm place. Meanwhile, put the pan back on the stovetop and simmer the pan juices for a few minutes, reducing the liquid if there is a lot, to make a tasty gravy.

5 Cut the lamb into thick slices—you'll find the meat falls away from the bone, so you may end up with more chunks than slices. Serve with creamy mashed potatoes and the wine gravy.

meatball curry with coriander breads and raita

This saucy dish isn't overly hot, so the cooling raita is not strictly necessary, but it does go well. Be sure you have plenty of chapattis on hand to scoop up all the lovely, spicy sauce.

SERVES 6

3 garlic cloves, peeled and quartered
2 hot red chili peppers, roughly chopped
1 thick slice of white bread
1 teaspoon cumin seeds
¼ cup mint leaves
1¾ lb lean ground lamb
1 egg, beaten
1–2 tablespoons vegetable oil
2 large onions, peeled and sliced
4 tomatoes, roughly chopped
2 cups hot lamb stock
3 tablespoons hot curry paste
sea salt and freshly ground black pepper

FOR THE RAITA:

1 cup thick, plain yogurt
1 hothouse cucumber, peeled and chopped
2 tablespoons chopped mint
1 garlic clove, peeled and crushed
pinch of sugar
pinch of salt
squeeze of lemon juice

FOR SERVING:

12 chapattis
2 tablespoons butter, melted
2 teaspoons ground coriander
small handful of mint leaves
1 lemon, cut into wedges

1 Put the garlic into a food processor with the chilies and tear in the bread. Add the cumin seeds and mint, and pulse until finely chopped. Transfer to a bowl and stir in the ground lamb, beaten egg, and plenty of salt and pepper. With damp hands, shape the mixture into walnut-sized balls.

2 Heat a splash of oil in a large, nonstick sauté pan and fry the meatballs in batches over a high heat for 3–4 minutes until nicely browned. Once all the meatballs are browned and set aside, add the onions to the pan and cook for 5–8 minutes until softened and golden. Add the tomatoes and cook for 2–3 minutes longer until they become a little pulpy.

3 Return the meatballs to the pan, along with the lamb stock and curry paste. Stir gently to mix. Bring to a boil and simmer gently for 30 minutes.

4 For the raita, combine the yogurt, cucumber, mint, and garlic in a bowl, then stir in the sugar, salt, and lemon juice to taste. Keep chilled.

5 When ready to serve, preheat a grill pan. Brush each chapatti with a little melted butter and sprinkle with ground coriander. Cook on the hot grill pan for 1 minute until speckled with brown. Divide the curry among warm bowls and scatter with mint leaves. Serve with the raita, chapattis, and lemon wedges.

thick-crust beef and ale pie

This is a wonderful old-fashioned steak pie with a delicious full flavor and a thick, firm pastry crust—arguably the best bit. Serve with mashed potatoes and English mustard.

SERVES 8

2 tablespoons olive oil

1 tablespoon butter

2 large onions, peeled and sliced

4 garlic cloves, peeled and chopped

1/4 cup all-purpose flour

3 1/4 lb beef for stew, cubed

4 cups stout or brown ale

3 tablespoons brown sugar

2 thyme sprigs

sea salt and freshly ground black pepper

FOR THE CRUST:

6 tablespoons lard, diced

1 2/3 cups all-purpose flour

1/4 teaspoon salt

1 egg, beaten, for glazing

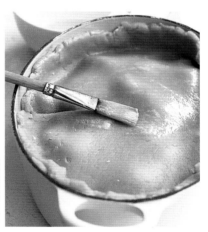

1   Heat the olive oil and butter in a stovetop-to-oven casserole, and cook the onions and garlic for 5 minutes until softened. Meanwhile, season the flour with salt and pepper and use to dust the beef.

2   Using a slotted spoon, lift out the onions and reserve. Brown the beef in the casserole in two batches. Return all the meat and the onions to the pot. Pour in the stout or ale, then stir in the sugar, thyme, and seasoning. Bring to a boil, partially cover, and simmer very gently for 2 hours.

3   Preheat the oven to 400°F. To make the crust, heat the lard with 1/2 cup water in a nonstick saucepan. Once boiling, shoot in the flour and salt, and stir with a wooden spoon until you have a smooth dough that forms a ball. Let cool for a few minutes.

4   Roll out the dough to a rough circle and use to cover the casserole. Brush the crust with the beaten egg and make a small hole in the middle so that steam can escape. Set the casserole on a baking sheet. Bake for 30 minutes, then lower the oven temperature to 325°F and bake for a further 1 hour until the crust is deep golden.

boiled ham in fragrant broth with sticky rice

An unusual twist on boiled ham, this is really fantastic. It is served with sticky rice and a ladleful of stock, although traditionalists can have their ham with mashed potatoes, if preferred.

SERVES 8

1 partially cooked ham, rump or butt portion,
* about 5 lb, preferably unsmoked*
4-inch piece of fresh ginger, roughly chopped
2 garlic cloves, peeled and roughly chopped
2 tomatoes, roughly chopped
1 bunch of green onions
2 star anise
2 cups sushi rice

1 Put the ham into a large pan with the ginger, garlic, and tomatoes. Cut off and reserve the green part of the green onions for serving. Slice the white part of the onions and add to the pan with the star anise. Cover with 3 quarts cold water.

2 Bring to a boil, then partially cover the pan and simmer very gently for 3 hours, skimming the surface frequently. Toward the end of the time, cook the rice according to the package directions.

3 Carefully lift the ham onto a board, reserving the liquid, and let rest for a couple of minutes. In the meantime, finely slice the green part of the green onions. Carve the ham into slices.

4 Divide the rice among eight warm, shallow bowls or soup plates and place the ham slices alongside. Strain the reserved liquid, then ladle some into each bowl and scatter on the onion greens (adding the star anise to a couple of bowls, if you like). Serve swiftly.

salt-and-pepper spareribs

For the popular Asian restaurant version of this dish, the spareribs are typically deep-fried, but I prefer to roast them. Serve with noodles or a simple salad.

SERVES 4

2 tablespoons all-purpose flour

1 tablespoon Chinese five spice powder

1/2 teaspoon salt

1/2 teaspoon crushed black pepper

2 1/4 lb pork spareribs

1 tablespoon sunflower oil

1 bunch of green onions, trimmed and
* thinly sliced*

1 hot red chili pepper, seeded and thinly sliced

1 garlic clove, peeled and minced

2 tablespoons soy sauce

1   Preheat the oven to 400°F. In a large bowl, mix together the flour, five spice powder, salt, and pepper. Roll each rib in the seasoned flour, then place side by side on a rack over a roasting pan.

2   Roast for 40–50 minutes, turning from time to time, until cooked through and beautifully browned. Arrange the ribs on a large platter.

3   Heat a wok, then add the oil. When it is hot, add the green onions and chili, and stir-fry over a high heat for 1 minute. Add the garlic and cook for 1 minute longer. Tip the contents of the wok over the ribs, then drizzle with the soy sauce. Serve immediately.

effortless entertaining

When it comes to dinner parties, I have five key points of advice to offer: plan in advance, keep it simple, prepare ahead, cut corners, and wash up as you go along. Stick to things you've cooked before or recipes that look easy. Once you've decided what you're going to cook, write a detailed shopping list, checking that you haven't missed anything.

Do as much as you can ahead of time. Choose a dessert than can be prepared the day before. Either make a cold dessert that sits overnight in the fridge or freezer, like Bellini gelatins (page 170), or frozen berry-yogurt pots (illustrated right), or one that goes into the oven as you sit down to the main course, such as oaty ginger-pear crisp (page 189). Then, once your guests have arrived, all you need to concentrate on is the main course. Similarly, opt for an easy appetizer, such as one of the ideas suggested here; each serves 6.

▲ **Italian antipasti**
Arrange 8 oz sliced cured meats, such as Milano salami, bresaola, and prosciutto, on a serving platter. Drizzle with a little olive oil, shave some Parmesan cheese over, and finish with a large grinding of black pepper. On a board, place a large wedge of Dolcelatte or Gorgonzola, a glassful of breadsticks, and a bowl of mixed olives with some toothpicks. Pass around some rosemary and garlic focaccia.

chilled fire-soup shots

Put a peeled, chopped hothouse cucumber into a food processor with 6 cups chopped tomatoes, 2 chopped hot red chili peppers, juice of 1 lime, and some salt. Blend until smooth and slushy. Pour into a cheesecloth-lined strainer set over a bowl and let drip for several hours—don't force it through or it will turn cloudy. Chill until required. Stir in a little minced cilantro and serve in shot glasses.

salmon pâté

Flake 4 oz roasted or baked salmon into a bowl and mix in 1 cup cream cheese, $1/2$ tsp horseradish cream, some chopped chives, and a squeeze of lemon juice. Add salt and pepper to taste. Serve with triangles of warm toast.

▲ frozen berry-yogurt pots

Prepare-ahead desserts are the key to easy entertaining. For this simple fruity ice, frozen summer berries and crumbled meringues are folded through creamy yogurt (see recipe, page 169). Make well in advance and freeze in freezerproof serving dishes, so you can serve straight from the freezer.

▲ pan-fried haloumi with fennel salad

Using a swivel peeler, shave 2 small fennel bulbs into wafer-thin slices; put into a bowl of chilled water and refrigerate for 1 hour to curl and crisp. For the dressing, whisk the juice of 1 orange with 4 tbsp olive oil, seasoning, and 2 tbsp chopped mint or tarragon. Cut 8 oz haloumi cheese into 6 slices, dust with seasoned flour, and fry in olive oil for 2 minutes on each side until golden. Drain the fennel and pile onto plates. Top with the haloumi, drizzle on the dressing, and serve swiftly.

eggplant, feta, and fava bean salad

This amazing salad is packed with Greek-style flavors and always makes me think of the sun. The avocado oil imparts a wonderful flavor, but you can substitute olive oil if you prefer. Serve with warm pita breads and a bowl of salad leaves for a summery lunch or supper.

SERVES 6

3 tablespoons olive oil

4 large eggplants, cut into cubes

1 cup shelled fresh fava beans or frozen baby
  lima beans

1 large red onion, peeled and thinly sliced

juice of 1 lemon

3 tablespoons avocado oil

8 oz baby plum tomatoes, halved

1 garlic clove, peeled and crushed

2 tablespoons minced black olives

2 tablespoons minced mint

14 oz feta cheese, roughly crumbled

sea salt and freshly ground black pepper

1 Preheat the oven to 425°F. Pour the olive oil into a shallow roasting pan and place in the oven to heat. Add the eggplant cubes and toss to coat in the hot oil, then roast for 30 minutes, turning from time to time, until cooked through and golden brown.

2 Meanwhile, add the fava or lima beans to a pan of boiling water, bring back to a boil, and simmer for 2 minutes or until tender. Drain well. If you have time, once the fava beans are cool enough to handle, pop them out of their skins. This is time-consuming, but worth it as the skins can be tough.

3 Tip the beans into a large bowl and add the red onion, lemon juice, 2 tablespoons of the avocado oil, and the tomatoes.

4 In another bowl, stir together the garlic, olives, mint, and remaining avocado oil. Lightly fold in the crumbled feta and set aside.

5 Once the eggplant is cooked, tip it into the bowl of tomatoes and beans, and mix well. Season with salt and pepper to taste, then set aside for 5 minutes, or let cool to room temperature. To serve, divide among serving plates and spoon the feta mixture on top.

Taleggio and thyme risotto

Risotto is a brilliant any-occasion dish. The addition of some soft, flavorsome Taleggio and fresh thyme makes this one rather special.

SERVES 6

4 tablespoons butter

1 red onion, peeled and minced

2 garlic cloves, peeled and minced

1 teaspoon thyme leaves

2 cups risotto rice, preferably carnaroli

1 1/4 cups Italian dry white wine

5 cups hot vegetable stock

1 lb Taleggio cheese, roughly chopped

1/4 cup chopped parsley

sea salt and freshly ground black pepper

1/4 cup freshly grated Parmesan cheese,
  for serving

1   Heat the butter in a large pan and cook the onion with the garlic and thyme leaves for 5 minutes until softened and golden. Add the rice and stir to coat with the butter.

2   Pour in the wine and bubble vigorously for 5 minutes or so until the liquid has been absorbed. Gradually add the stock, roughly one-fourth at a time, stirring and simmering until each batch has been absorbed before adding the next. Total cooking time will be about 20 minutes.

3   Remove the risotto from the heat and stir through the Taleggio and parsley. Check the seasoning, adding salt and pepper to taste. Divide among warm serving bowls and top each with a sprinkling of freshly grated Parmesan.

red pepper and fontina couscous cake

This makes a lovely light lunch, perfect with an arugula and tomato salad and some chilled red wine. In order to make the couscous hold together, it needs to be slightly over-moistened, which is why there is more stock than usual.

SERVES 4

1³/₄ cups couscous
2 cups hot vegetable stock
juice of 1 lime
2 tablespoons olive oil
¹/₂ cup bottled roasted red peppers, drained and
    cut into ¹/₂-inch-wide strips
8 oz fontina or Gruyère cheese, cut into
    small dice
1 egg, beaten
¹/₄ cup snipped chives
freshly ground black pepper

1   Put the couscous into a large, heatproof bowl. Stir together the vegetable stock, lime juice, and a large grinding of black pepper, then pour over the couscous. Let soak for 15 minutes until all the stock has been absorbed.

2   Heat a splash of the olive oil in a 9-inch nonstick frying pan. Stir the peppers, cheese, egg, and chives into the couscous, then tip into the pan and pat down well into a cake. Cook over a gentle heat for 15 minutes, without touching, until the base is crisp and golden.

3   Carefully slide the couscous cake onto a plate, then turn upside-down back into the pan, adding the rest of the oil if needed. Cook for 10 minutes or so longer until the other side is golden. Slide back onto the plate and cut into wedges to serve.

cheese-and-onion baked potatoes

These are the most delicious baked potatoes I have ever eaten. Simple, but sumptuously tasty. I keep the red onions raw, because I like the freshness they offer, but you can soften them first in a little olive oil if you prefer.

SERVES 6

6 russet potatoes, each about 9 oz
1 tablespoon olive oil
coarse sea salt, for sprinkling
2 small red onions, peeled and minced
$^3/_4$ cup shredded Gruyère or Emmental cheese
$^3/_4$ cup shredded aged Cheddar cheese
$1^1/_4$ cups sour cream
sea salt and freshly ground black pepper

1 Preheat the oven to 400°F. Pierce the potatoes in several places with a fork, then rub with the olive oil and sprinkle with salt. Bake directly on the middle oven rack for 1 hour and 20 minutes, turning from time to time.

2 To check that the potatoes are cooked, wrap them in a clean dish towel and give them a gentle squeeze—they should feel soft. Keeping each potato wrapped in the dish towel, hit each one with your fist, so that the skin splits (this looks more natural than cutting them open).

3 Scoop the fluffy flesh out of the potatoes and place in a bowl. Stir in the onions, shredded cheeses, sour cream, and some salt and pepper. Roughly pile back into the potato shells. Place on a baking sheet and bake for 30–40 minutes until golden brown. Serve hot, with salad or baked beans.

4 lunchboxes and snacks

sticky lemon chicken wings

Easy and delicious, baked chicken wings are the ideal late-night snack, eaten hot from the oven. Or, you can eat them cold the next day, packed in a lunchbox or picnic basket.

SERVES 4

12 large chicken wings
2 tablespoons butter, melted
grated zest and juice of 1 lemon
1 teaspoon chili powder
¼ teaspoon sea salt

1   Preheat the oven to 400°F. Using a strong pair of scissors, snip the tip off each wing and discard.

2   Mix together the melted butter, lemon zest and juice, chili powder, and salt.

3   Arrange the chicken wings on a rack set over a roasting pan and brush both sides with the lemony butter. Roast for 30–40 minutes, turning and basting once or twice, until golden brown.

prosciutto and mozzarella focaccia

Here, a classic focaccia dough is reinforced with potato to give a gorgeous texture that really satisfies. Cut into wedges and eat in place of a regular sandwich.

SERVES 6

2 cups peeled and cubed russet or all-purpose
   potatoes
9 cups Italian "00" white bread flour
¹⁄₄-oz envelope quick-rising active dry yeast
6 oz thinly sliced prosciutto, roughly torn
11 oz mozzarella cheese, drained and diced

6 sun-dried tomatoes in oil, drained and diced
1 teaspoon salt
2 tablespoons olive oil
2 tablespoons Italian or French chili oil (not
   Asian-style)
1 teaspoon coarse sea salt
1 rosemary sprig, roughly chopped

1 Cook the potatoes in a large pan of boiling salted water for 15 minutes until tender. Drain well and turn into a large bowl. Mash thoroughly, then let cool.

2 Tip the mash onto a lightly floured surface and add the flour, yeast, ham, mozzarella, sun-dried tomatoes, and fine salt. Make a well in the center, and add the olive oil and 1¾ cups warm water. Gradually incorporate the dry ingredients into the liquid and mix to a soft dough, adding a little more warm water if needed.

3 Knead the dough on the floured surface for at least 5 minutes until smooth. Roll out to a large oval shape about ½ inch thick. Transfer to a baking sheet, cover with a clean dish towel, and let rise for an hour or so until doubled in size.

4 Preheat the oven to 400°F. Using your fingertips, make indentations about ¾ inch deep all over the surface of the dough. Drizzle with the chili oil and sprinkle with sea salt and rosemary. Bake for 35–40 minutes until risen and golden brown. Let cool for a few minutes before slicing.

chicken palm pies

These little pies are so-named because they fit neatly in the palm of your hand. They are perfect for lunchboxes, and ideal for freezing.

Illustrated on previous page

MAKES 12

3 oz cubed pancetta (Italian bacon), or 3 thick
 bacon slices cut into small strips
4 large skinless, boneless chicken thighs
1 teaspoon cornstarch
1 small onion, peeled and minced

1 teaspoon chopped sage
1/2 cup chicken stock
squeeze of lemon juice
1 1/4 lb refrigerated piecrust dough
1 egg yolk
sea salt and freshly ground black pepper

1 Cook the pancetta or bacon in a large, nonstick frying pan for 3–4 minutes until crisp and golden brown. Remove with a slotted spoon and set aside.

2 Cut the chicken thighs into 1/2-inch pieces and dust with the cornstarch. Add to the frying pan along with the onion and cook for 8–10 minutes until well browned and cooked through, adding the sage for the last minute of the cooking time.

3 Stir in the stock and bring to a boil. Season with salt and pepper, and add a squeeze of lemon juice to taste, then let cool.

4 Preheat the oven to 400°F. Roll out three-fourths of the dough. Cut out twelve 6-inch disks and use to line a 12-cup muffin pan, letting the excess dough hang over the edges. Roll out the remaining dough and cut out twelve 3-inch disks for lids.

5 Stir the pancetta or bacon into the chicken mixture, then divide among the pastry shells. Dampen the inside edges of the pastry shells with a little water. Top each with a pastry lid, then fold the edges of the pastry shell over the lid and press together to seal. Cut a small hole in the top of each pie.

6 Mix together the egg yolk and 1/4 teaspoon salt. Brush this over the pies, then bake for 20 minutes until the pastry is crisp and well glazed. Let cool. Wrap individually in wax paper to pack into lunchboxes.

sesame chicken and noodle salad

This Asian-style salad is a tasty, satisfying alternative to lunchbox sandwiches. Either buy cooked chicken portions from the deli counter, or use chicken leftover from a roast.

SERVES 2

3 oz flat rice noodles
6 oz cooked boneless chicken breast
1 tablespoon soy sauce
2 tablespoons sweet chili sauce
4 green onions, trimmed and minced
2 teaspoons sesame seeds, toasted
1/2 teaspoon toasted sesame oil
handful of cilantro leaves, roughly torn
sea salt and freshly ground black pepper

1 Put the rice noodles into a heatproof bowl. Cover with boiling water and let soak for 5 minutes.

2 Meanwhile, remove the skin from the chicken breast and cut the meat into fine strips. Place in a bowl, add the soy and chili sauces, and toss to mix.

3 Drain the rice noodles, refresh under cold running water, and drain thoroughly. Add to the chicken strips along with the green onions, sesame seeds, and sesame oil. Toss well and season with salt and pepper to taste. Add the cilantro leaves.

4 Either serve at once or pack into plastic containers for lunchboxes.

wraps and sandwiches

With the fantastic selection of breads now readily available—and a little imagination—the humble sandwich can be turned into a delicious and satisfying meal. I've become a real fan of flatbreads, and there are plenty to choose from, including flour tortillas, pita breads, naans, and chapattis.

All flatbreads become a little softer and easier to roll if you heat them very briefly, either in a dry frying pan or for a few seconds in a microwave. Once filled and rolled, wrap in wax paper, twisting the ends to secure. When ready to eat, peel down the paper like a banana skin.

There's no limit to the variety of fillings. Try grilled eggplant slices with feta and tzatziki; prosciutto and Taleggio cheese with torn basil; sliced roast beef with peppery arugula and horseradish cream; or cold roast pork (page 160) with a little redcurrant jelly—my favorite. Or try one of the following original ideas.

▲ **spicy omelet chapatti**
To make 1, heat 1 tsp oil in a small frying pan, add 1 chopped, hot green chili pepper, 1 chopped green onion, and 3 halved cherry tomatoes, and cook for 2–3 minutes. Stir in 1 tsp garam masala and cook for 1 minute. Swirl in 1 lightly beaten egg and cook until the base is set. Flip the omelet over and cook for a minute on the other side. Place the omelet on top of a chapatti and spread 1 tbsp sweet chili sauce over. Roll up and wrap in wax paper, then foil.

chicken tikka wraps

To serve 4, cut 4 small skinless, boneless chicken breast halves into 1/2-inch strips. Coat in 2/3 cup plain yogurt mixed with 1 crushed garlic clove, 1 tsp ground cumin, 1/4 tsp cayenne, 1/4 tsp ground turmeric, and 1/2 tsp salt. Broil on a foil-lined pan, turning, until cooked through. Divide among 4 warm flour tortillas, scatter on some shredded iceberg lettuce, and roll up tightly. Wrap in wax paper. Serve with lemon wedges.

skewered lamb and eggplant pitas

To serve 2, combine 1/4 chopped hothouse cucumber, 2 roughly chopped tomatoes, and a handful of chopped mint in a bowl. Squeeze in a little lemon juice, add a drizzle of olive oil, and season well. Toast 2 pita breads in the toaster or under the broiler. Split open and spoon 2 tbsp store-bought eggplant dip into each. Slide the meat from 2 cooked lamb skewers (bought from the deli counter) into each pita and spoon the tomato and cucumber salad on top. Wrap in foil.

▲ crusty Tex-Mex roll

To make 1, slice the top 1/2–3/4 inch off a crusty bread roll and remove most of the bread from the inside, leaving a layer about 1/2 inch thick inside the crust. Fill with a few spoonfuls of canned refried beans, 1/2 minced hot green chili pepper, a handful of shredded Cheddar cheese, and a dollop of sour cream. Replace the top of the roll and wrap in plastic wrap or wax paper. Leave for an hour before eating.

potato pasties

It's worth making a lot of these terrific pasties, as they freeze brilliantly—simply pack them in pairs in small bags. Once thawed, you can warm them up in the oven.

MAKES 10

1¾ lb russet or all-purpose potatoes, peeled
  and cubed
1 tablespoon olive oil
2 shallots, peeled and minced
1 garlic clove, peeled and minced

1 teaspoon cayenne
1 teaspoon prepared English mustard
2 cups shredded Cheddar cheese
7 oz phyllo pastry, thawed if frozen
2 tablespoons butter, melted
sea salt and freshly ground black pepper

1 Cook the potatoes in a pan of boiling salted water for 15 minutes until tender.

2 Meanwhile, heat the olive oil in a large, nonstick frying pan and gently cook the shallots and garlic for 2–3 minutes. Drain the potatoes well and add to the frying pan, mashing them roughly with a fork. Let cool.

3 Preheat the oven to 400°F. Stir the cayenne, mustard, and cheese into the potato mixture, and season generously with salt and pepper.

4 Cut the sheets of phyllo pastry to make twenty 12- by 3½-inch strips. To make each pasty, place two strips of pastry on the work surface, overlapping them at right angles to form an L shape. Spoon some of the potato mixture onto the overlapped corner, then fold over the two strips alternately to enclose the filling. Turn over, then fold the two strips back over so that you make a square parcel with all four sides enclosed.

5 Brush the pasties lightly with melted butter and transfer to a nonstick baking sheet. Bake for 20 minutes until crisp and golden brown. Serve warm, or cool on a wire rack before wrapping in wax paper or foil.

butternut squash and Parmesan muffins

The combination of butternut squash and Parmesan not only tastes delicious but also makes these easy muffins nutritious and satisfying. Eat within a day of baking.

MAKES 12

1 small butternut squash, about 14 oz,
  peeled, seeded, and diced
1 red onion, peeled and minced
1 tablespoon olive oil
6 tablespoons butter, melted
1¼ cups freshly grated Parmesan cheese, plus
  a little extra for sprinkling
1⅔ cups self-rising flour
4 eggs, beaten
3–4 tablespoons milk
sea salt and freshly ground black pepper

1 Preheat the oven to 400°F. Place the squash and onion on a baking sheet and drizzle with the olive oil. Season with salt and pepper. Bake for 15 minutes until tender. Roughly mash on the baking sheet.

2 Lower the oven temperature to 350°F. Line a 12-cup muffin pan with squares of parchment paper (pushed in roughly) or with paper muffin cases.

3 Spoon the pumpkin and onion mixture into a large bowl and stir in the melted butter, Parmesan, flour, eggs, milk, and some salt and pepper to make a thick, lumpy batter. Divide the batter among the muffin cups and sprinkle a little extra Parmesan on top of each one. Bake for 20–25 minutes until golden and just firm.

4 Transfer to a wire rack to cool. Serve warm or let cool completely before packing into lunchboxes.

gorgeous cranberry cookies

These scrumptious cookies really deserve their name—they're crunchy with a lovely, buttery flavor and little nuggets of chewy dried cranberry. Store in an airtight container.

MAKES 24

1¹/₂ sticks unsalted butter, at room temperature
³/₄ cup sugar
finely grated zest of 1 large orange
2 egg yolks
¹/₂ cup ground almonds
¹/₃ cup dried cranberries or cherries
1²/₃ cup self-rising flour
2 tablespoons milk

1 Preheat the oven to 325°F. Using an electric mixer, beat together the butter and sugar until pale and creamy.

2 Stir in the orange zest, egg yolks, ground almonds, dried cranberries, and flour. Mix well together, then roll into walnut-sized balls.

3 Place on a baking sheet, spaced well apart, and flatten each ball slightly with your hand. Brush with milk, then bake for 18–20 minutes until golden.

4 After removing from the oven, let the cookies firm up on the baking sheet for 5 minutes before transferring to a wire rack to cool.

caramel-ripple brownies

These rich brownies are fantastic served with coffee. As they are quite dense, cut them into small squares and wrap in foil for lunchboxes.

MAKES 16

4 oz (4 squares) bittersweet chocolate

7 tablespoons unsalted butter

2 eggs, beaten

2/3 cup packed light brown sugar

1/3 cup all-purpose flour

FOR THE CARAMEL RIPPLE:

1 cup cream cheese

3 1/2 tablespoons dark brown sugar

few drops of pure vanilla extract

1 egg

1 Preheat the oven to 325°F. Line an 8-inch-square shallow cake pan with parchment paper.

2 Break the chocolate into a heatproof bowl and add the butter. Set over a pan of gently simmering water and melt, stirring from time to time.

3 Meanwhile, prepare the caramel ripple mixture. Combine the cream cheese, brown sugar, vanilla, and egg in a bowl and mix well until evenly blended. Set aside.

4 Stir the eggs and sugar into the chocolate mixture, then sift the flour on top and gently fold in.

5 Spoon half of the chocolate mixture into the prepared pan, then alternately dollop teaspoonfuls of the caramel mixture and the remaining chocolate mixture on top. Using a chopstick or skewer, lightly ripple together to make a marbled top.

6 Bake for 25–30 minutes until just set. Let cool in the pan for 5–10 minutes before cutting into squares. Transfer to a wire rack to cool completely.

lemon custard tarts

Based on yummy traditional Portuguese tarts, these sweet and lemony mouthfuls, paired with a cup of hot black coffee, will really perk you up. Fortunately they are not too fragile to tuck into school lunchboxes, too.

MAKES 24

12 oz puff pastry, thawed if frozen
1 vanilla bean
1¼ cups milk
1 egg

1 egg yolk
¼ cup granulated sugar
3 tablespoons all-purpose flour
grated zest and juice of ½ lemon
confectioners' sugar, for dusting (optional)

1 Preheat the oven to 400°F. Roll out the pastry as thinly as possible, then cut out twenty-four 2¾-inch rounds. Use to line two 12-cup mini muffin pans.

2 Fill each pastry shell with a dense ball of foil. Bake for 10–15 minutes until crisp and light golden. Remove the foil and set aside. Lower the oven temperature to 325°F.

3 To make the filling, split the vanilla bean lengthwise and place in a saucepan with the milk. Heat until almost boiling, then set aside for 10 minutes. Meanwhile, beat together the egg, egg yolk, granulated sugar, and flour in a bowl until smooth.

4 Remove the vanilla bean from the warm milk, then gradually pour onto the egg mixture. Return to a clean pan and stir over a medium heat until simmering. When the mixture begins to simmer, beat it quite vigorously to get rid of any lumps. Stir in the lemon zest and juice.

5 Divide the lemon filling among the pastry shells. Bake the tarts for 10–15 minutes until the custard filling has set. Leave in the pans for a few minutes, then carefully transfer to a wire rack to cool. Dust with confectioners' sugar before serving, if you like.

raspberry and almond slice

Here's a quick, rather rustic version of a traditional English Bakewell tart. The classic tart derived from Bakewell pudding, which tended to be soggy. I'd rather have one of these slices any day.

SERVES 8

1¼ lb refrigerated piecrust dough
4 tablespoons butter, at room temperature
¼ cup granulated sugar
1 medium egg
1¼ cups ground almonds
few drops of pure vanilla extract
1 cup raspberries
¼ cup sliced almonds
1 tablespoon confectioners' sugar

1   Preheat the oven to 400°F. Roll out the pastry to a 12- by 8-inch rectangle—don't worry if the edges aren't straight, as that's part of the charm of this tart. Transfer to a nonstick baking sheet and prick in several places. Bake for 5 minutes until set.

2   Meanwhile, using an electric mixer, beat the butter and granulated sugar together until pale and fluffy. Stir in the egg, ground almonds, and vanilla to make a stiff paste.

3   Spread the almond paste on top of the pastry, leaving a ½-inch border clear on all sides. Gently press the raspberries into the paste. Scatter the almonds over the raspberries and sift the confectioners' sugar on top. Bake for 20–25 minutes until puffed and golden.

4   Leave on the baking sheet for a few minutes, then carefully transfer to a wire rack to cool. Slice and serve warm or at room temperature.

moist mango and maple cake

This sweet and fruity teatime quick bread is incredibly easy to make. It's reminiscent of a carrot cake, so I've topped it with a delicious cream-cheese frosting. Wrap thick slices in wax paper for picnics and lunchboxes.

SERVES 8

$1/2$ cup (1 stick) butter

$2/3$ cup packed light brown sugar

$1/3$ cup maple syrup

1 cup all-purpose flour

$3/4$ cup whole-wheat flour

2 teaspoons baking powder

1 tablespoon ground cinnamon

2 ripe mangoes, peeled, seeded, and finely chopped

1 cup roughly chopped pecans

FOR THE FROSTY TOPPING:

grated zest and juice of 1 small orange

1 cup cream cheese

$1/2$ cup confectioners' sugar, sifted

1 Preheat the oven to 325°F. Gently melt the butter, brown sugar, and maple syrup together in a small pan.

2 In a large bowl, mix together the flours, baking powder, cinnamon, mangoes, and pecans. Stir in the melted syrup mixture.

3 Spoon the batter into a nonstick loaf pan that is about 6$1/2$ by 4 inches and 3$1/4$ inches deep. Bake for 1–1$1/4$ hours until a skewer inserted into the center of the cake comes out clean.

4 Let the cake cool in the pan for 5 minutes, then unmold onto a wire rack to cool completely.

5 For the topping, mix together the orange zest, cream cheese, and confectioners' sugar with enough of the orange juice to make a smooth, thick paste. Spread thickly over the top of the cooled cake. Cut into slices to serve.

5 just for two

tiger shrimp tagliatelle

The perfect choice for a romantic supper for two, this is best made in the summer when tomatoes are at their tastiest. I've used fresh tagliatelle here, but you could always use dried pasta—add to a pan of boiling salted water at the beginning of step 1, and the sauce will be ready in the time it takes the pasta to cook.

SERVES 2

1 tablespoon olive oil
1 garlic clove, peeled and thinly sliced
3 ripe tomatoes, chopped
grated zest of 1 small lemon
squeeze of lemon juice
pinch of sugar
pinch of dried chili flakes
8 oz cooked, peeled tiger shrimp
9 oz fresh tagliatelle
2 tablespoons chopped flat-leaf parsley
sea salt and freshly ground black pepper

1   Heat the olive oil in a small frying pan and cook the garlic for 1 minute until beginning to soften. Add the tomatoes and simmer gently for 5 minutes until they become pulpy.

2   Add the lemon zest and juice, the sugar, chili flakes, and seasoning to taste. Stir to mix. Add the shrimp and cook gently for a couple of minutes until heated through.

3   Meanwhile, cook the pasta in a large pan of boiling salted water according to the package directions until *al dente* (tender, but firm to the bite).

4   Drain the pasta well and return to the pan. Add the shrimp sauce and parsley, and toss to mix, then divide between warm bowls and serve.

grilled tuna with fiery tomato salsa

Fresh tuna has a meaty texture and a mild flavor that's well matched with a wicked little salsa like this one. Serve with summery salad leaves and some crusty bread.

SERVES 2

2 ripe tomatoes, roughly chopped
1 shallot, peeled and thinly sliced
1 small garlic clove, peeled and very thinly sliced
1 hot green chili pepper, minced
pinch of dried chili flakes
juice of 1 lime
2 tablespoons olive oil
2 fresh tuna steaks, each about 6 oz
1 teaspoon cracked black peppercorns
2 tablespoons chopped mint or cilantro
sea salt and freshly ground black pepper

1 Mix the tomatoes, shallot, garlic, chili pepper, and chili flakes together in a bowl. Stir in the lime juice, 1 tablespoon olive oil, and some salt and pepper. Set aside at room temperature for at least 5 minutes, or up to an hour.

2 Preheat a ridged grill pan. Rub the rest of the olive oil over the tuna steaks. Sprinkle with the peppercorns and press them in lightly with your fingertips.

3 Cook the tuna for 2–3 minutes on each side until nicely browned but still slightly pink in the center. Place on two warm plates. Stir the mint into the salsa, then spoon onto and alongside the tuna.

potato-stuffed squab chickens

I do like little squab chickens, especially for a smart supper for two. They don't have the flavor of a fully grown chicken, but take very well to some robust seasonings, such as lemon and rosemary, with a little chili kick. You can also use Cornish game hens.

SERVES 2

1 russet or all-purpose potato, about 8 oz,
  peeled and diced
1 tablespoon olive oil
3 rosemary sprigs
1 shallot, peeled and sliced
1 garlic clove, peeled and minced
pinch of dried chili flakes
1 lemon
2 squab chickens, each about 1¼ lb
2 tablespoons butter, at room temperature
salt and freshly ground black pepper

1   Cook the potato in a pan of boiling salted water for 10–15 minutes until tender.

2   Preheat the oven to 400°F. Heat the oil in a small frying pan. Strip the leaves off one of the rosemary sprigs, roughly chop, and add to the pan along with the shallot and garlic. Cook for 5 minutes until softened, then remove from the heat and transfer to a shallow bowl.

3   Drain the potato, add to the bowl, and crush roughly. Add the chili flakes, then grate in about half the zest from the lemon. Add salt and pepper, and let cool.

4   Meanwhile, cut four thin slices off the lemon. Loosen the skin on the breast of each chicken and slide a rosemary sprig and two lemon slices between the meat and the skin.

5   Spoon the mash into the chicken cavities, then rub the butter over the breasts. Season with salt and pepper, and place side by side in a small roasting pan. Roast for 50 minutes to 1 hour until crisp, golden, and cooked through. Serve whole, with simple vegetables.

hot lamb baguette with mint and lime

I love a hot sandwich and, although steak with fried onions and melting cheese is pretty hard to beat, this minty lamb version has an altogether fresher, more vibrant flavor. I spread the bread with red-currant jelly because it works beautifully with the mint and lime, but horseradish cream makes a surprisingly delicious alternative.

SERVES 2

4 thin, boneless lamb leg steaks
1 teaspoon olive oil
2 pieces of baguette, each about 8 inches long
2 teaspoons red-currant jelly
1 garlic clove, halved
$1/_3$ cup mint leaves
1 lime, cut into wedges
sea salt and freshly ground black pepper

1   Preheat a ridged grill pan. Brush the lamb with the olive oil and cook in the hot pan for about 2 minutes on each side.

2   Meanwhile, split open the piece of baguette and spread the red-currant jelly on the bases.

3   Transfer the lamb steaks to a large plate and rub with the cut surface of the garlic. Season the lamb with salt and pepper to taste, then place two steaks inside each baguette. Roughly tear in the mint leaves, squeeze in some lime juice, and serve warm.

Thai beef salad

This classic salad, which originated in northeast Thailand, is a standard in Thai restaurants but is very easy to make at home. The beef is only seared on the outside and should be served very rare, so don't be tempted to overcook it. Some steamed rice and an icy beer are all you need for a delicious and rather elegant supper.
Illustrated on previous page

SERVES 2

9-oz piece of beef tenderloin or filet mignon
1 teaspoon vegetable oil
juice of 1 lime
2 tablespoons Thai fish sauce
1 teaspoon sugar
1 shallot, peeled and very thinly sliced
1 garlic clove, peeled and minced
2 tablespoons roughly chopped mint or cilantro
1 Thai chili pepper, thinly sliced
1 romaine heart, roughly torn
1 cup bean sprouts

1   Heat a small, nonstick frying pan. Rub the beef with the oil and place in the hot pan. Cook over a very high heat for 5 minutes, turning, until well browned all over. Transfer to a plate and let rest for 5 minutes.

2   For the dressing, mix the lime juice, fish sauce, and sugar together in a bowl, then stir in the shallot, garlic, mint, and chili.

3   Pile the torn lettuce onto two serving plates, then scatter on the bean sprouts. Thinly slice the beef and arrange on top. Spoon the dressing over the salad and serve.

stir-fried pork and ginger noodles

A zingy little stir-fry, this is cooked and on the table in under 10 minutes. It is a standard of my friend and fellow food writer, Jenny White, who regularly fixes this in our lunch break.

SERVES 2

1 tablespoon sunflower oil
8 oz pork tenderloin, cut in strips
1½-inch piece of fresh ginger, peeled
* and shredded*
4 green onions, trimmed and shredded
1 hot red chili pepper, seeded and thinly sliced
1 lb vacuum-packed udon noodles
2 tablespoons soy sauce
juice of 1 small orange
1 teaspoon Asian chili oil
1 teaspoon wine vinegar
handful of basil leaves

1   Heat a wok, then add the oil. When hot, add the pork strips and stir-fry for 5 minutes. Add the ginger, green onions, chili pepper, and noodles, and cook for 2 minutes longer.

2   Mix the soy sauce, orange juice, chili oil, and vinegar together in a bowl, then pour into the pan. Toss together well and cook for 1 minute or so until piping hot.

3   Add the basil leaves and toss to mix, then divide the stir-fry between warm bowls and serve.

sausage and lentil casserole

I always keep a variety of lentils in stock as they're fantastic for stews and soups. The French lentille de Puy is considered to be better than most, and while it does have a lovely texture and flavor, if you're serving this dish for supper, you can use everyday brown or green lentils.

SERVES 2
1 teaspoon olive oil
6 large, fresh pork sausages
1 small onion, peeled and roughly chopped
2 garlic cloves, peeled and roughly chopped
³/₄ cup lentilles de Puy
2¹/₂ cups hot chicken stock
1 large tomato, roughly chopped
1 teaspoon balsamic vinegar
3 tablespoons chopped flat-leaf parsley
sea salt and freshly ground black pepper

1   Heat the olive oil in a sauté pan and cook the sausages, turning from time to time, for 5–8 minutes until golden on all sides. Add the onion and garlic, and cook for 2–3 minutes until beginning to soften.

2   Add the lentils, stock, and chopped tomato. Bring to a boil, then cover and simmer very gently for 40–45 minutes until the lentils are tender and most of the stock has been absorbed.

3   Stir in the balsamic vinegar and parsley, and add salt and pepper to taste. Spoon into warm bowls and serve with crusty bread.

freezer dinners for two

Sometimes after a hectic day, you just don't have the time or energy to cook. But this doesn't mean you have to resort to store-bought meals or fast food. With a little forward planning, you can always have an appetizing meal on hand in your freezer. Casseroles, stews, curries, soups, and pasta sauces are perfect for making in larger quantities and freezing. All of the recipes featured here serve 4, so make one for dinner, eat two portions right away, and freeze the rest to enjoy at a later date.

Let the food cool completely before transferring to a suitable freezer container, and make sure it has a well-fitting lid—food left open in the freezer will suffer from freezer burn, and the texture and flavor will be ruined. Plastic food boxes, foil takeout cartons, and sealed freezer bags are all ideal for freezing food. Freeze for up to 2 months. Thaw overnight in the fridge and reheat thoroughly to serve.

▲ Greek-style baked lamb with potatoes

Heat 2 tbsp olive oil in a roasting pan and fry 1 large sliced onion and 4 chopped garlic cloves for 3–4 minutes; push to one side. Add 4 bone-in lamb leg or shoulder steaks and brown over a high heat for 2–3 minutes on each side. Add 3 cups peeled, diced potatoes and cook for 3 minutes. Add 14 oz canned cherry or crushed tomatoes, 1¼ cups lamb stock, a bay leaf, 1 tsp dried oregano, and 12 pitted black olives. Bake at 375°F for 30–40 minutes until the potatoes are tender.

baked pork and beans

In a stovetop-to-oven casserole, fry 1½ lb diced pork fatback for 5 minutes; remove with a slotted spoon. Fry 1 large diced onion and 2 chopped garlic cloves until tender. Stir in 2½ cups hard cider, ⅔ cup tomato purée, 2 tbsp sun-dried tomato paste, 1 tbsp molasses, 1 tbsp brown sugar, 1 tsp black mustard seeds, the fatback, and a drained 14-oz can blackeye peas. Season, then cover and cook at 325°F for 1–1½ hours.

▲ zucchini and mint soup

Heat 3 tbsp butter in a large saucepan and fry 1 minced onion for 5 minutes until softened. Add 12oz sliced zucchini and cook for 2–3 minutes. Pour in 3 cups vegetable stock and bring to a simmer. Season, then cover and simmer for 10–15 minutes until the zucchini are tender. Stir in a big handful of chopped mint. Let cool slightly, then blend until smooth. Heat through gently for serving.

▲ quick coq au vin

Heat 2 tbsp oil in a large sauté pan. Fry 8 large chicken thighs for 4 minutes on each side; remove. Add 4 chopped bacon slices, 8 peeled shallots, and 8oz halved cremini mushrooms; fry, stirring, for 5 minutes. Discard excess fat, then return the chicken. Add 2 tbsp brandy and cook for 1 minute, then stir in 1¼ cups red wine, 1 cup chicken stock, 2 tbsp tomato paste, and a bay leaf. Season, then cover and simmer gently for 15 minutes. Uncover and cook for 10 minutes longer.

ricotta and basil frittata

This flat omelet offers a delicious pairing of two key Italian ingredients—ricotta and basil. I've used the traditional southern Italian method of tearing some fresh white bread into the beaten eggs to give the frittata a firm, almost cakelike texture. Serve with a tomato and red onion salad, and good crusty bread.

SERVES 2

2 tablespoons olive oil
5 eggs
2 slices of white bread, crusts removed
1 garlic clove, peeled and crushed
1/4 cup minced basil
2/3 cup ricotta cheese
sea salt and freshly ground black pepper

1 Preheat the broiler. Heat a splash of the olive oil in an 8-inch frying pan. Beat the eggs in a large bowl, then tear in the white bread and season with salt and pepper. Pour into the pan and cook very gently for 5 minutes.

2 Meanwhile, in a mortar and pestle, pound together the garlic and basil to make a paste. Stir in the remaining olive oil and season with salt and pepper.

3 Drop spoonfuls of the ricotta onto the fritatta, then drizzle with the basil dressing. Cook for a further 2–3 minutes until the frittata is almost set, then finish cooking under the broiler for 3–4 minutes until completely set and golden brown.

4 Slide the frittata out of the pan onto a board and cut into wedges to serve.

lima bean and mozzarella burgers

These juicy, succulent bean burgers have delicious pockets of molten mozzarella inside. Lima beans are the perfect beans for burgers as they have a lovely creamy texture and combine well with aromatics, such as green onions and garlic.

SERVES 2

4 green onions, trimmed and thickly sliced
1 garlic clove, peeled and thickly sliced
14 oz canned baby lima beans, drained
2 cups fresh white bread crumbs
5 oz mozzarella cheese, drained and diced
1 egg yolk
pinch of cayenne
2–3 tablespoons vegetable oil
sea salt and freshly ground black pepper

FOR SERVING:
2 crusty bread rolls, split open
1 ripe tomato, sliced
mayonnaise

1 Put the green onions and garlic into a food processor and blend until finely chopped. Add the beans and blend again to form a coarse purée. Add the bread crumbs, mozzarella, egg yolk, cayenne, and some salt and pepper. Pulse to form a stiff paste.

2 Shape the mixture into two burgers. Heat the oil in a heavy, nonstick frying pan. Shallow-fry the burgers for 3–4 minutes on each side until golden—the cheese may ooze out and make the burgers stick a little, so make sure you use a good nonstick pan.

3 Drain the burgers on paper towels. Serve in the crusty rolls with a few slices of tomato and a big dollop of mayonnaise.

6 family feasts

roast salmon and goat cheese salad

This is a smashing summery salad. With its mix of pinks and greens, it looks gorgeous when casually presented on a large platter. Prepare all the elements, such as the crostini and salmon, ahead of time and just assemble when ready to serve.

SERVES 12

1 baguette, cut into ½-inch slices

3–4 tablespoons olive oil

6 pieces of salmon fillet, each about 9 oz

2 heads romaine, sliced or torn into large pieces

1 large hothouse cucumber, peeled and thinly
  sliced

⅓ cup mint leaves, roughly torn

¼ cup snipped chives

7 oz cooked beets, thinly sliced (about 1 cup)

14 oz medium-soft goat cheese

FOR THE DRESSING:

3 tablespoons olive oil

1 tablespoon red wine vinegar

pinch of sugar

sea salt and freshly ground black pepper

1   Preheat the oven to 425°F. Arrange the slices of bread on baking sheets and brush lightly with olive oil, then sprinkle with a little sea salt. Bake for 10–12 minutes until golden brown. Let cool on a wire rack, then pile these crostini on a serving board.

2   Arrange the salmon fillets on a baking sheet. Brush with a little olive oil and season with salt and pepper. Bake for 12–15 minutes until golden and just cooked. Let cool.

3   Scatter the lettuce on a large serving platter. Add the cucumber, mint, chives, and beets. Crumble on the goat cheese. Flake the salmon and scatter on top.

4   Mix together the dressing ingredients and drizzle over the salad. Serve fairly swiftly, with the crostini on the side.

smoked salmon tart

This is perfect for a family feast. Make two tarts the day before and keep in a cool, dry place—not the fridge or the pastry will go soggy. Serve with a simple salad for an elegant lunch.

SERVES 6

1²/₃ cups all-purpose flour
¹/₂ teaspoon salt
9 tablespoons chilled butter, diced
1 teaspoon dried chili flakes
2 cups heavy cream

2 eggs
2 egg yolks
¹/₂ cup freshly grated Parmesan cheese
7 oz smoked salmon, roughly torn
   into strips
sea salt and freshly ground black pepper

1 Preheat the oven to 400°F. Place the flour, salt, butter, and chili flakes in a food processor and blend until the mixtures forms fine crumbs. Pour in 3 tablespoons very cold water and pulse again briefly, to form a firm dough.

2 Roll out the pastry on a floured surface and use to line an 8¹/₂-inch loose-bottomed tart pan. Use a rolling pin to lift the pastry into the pan. Press the pastry well into the sides, then trim away excess pastry overhanging the rim.

3 Prick the bottom of the pastry shell with a fork, then fill with crumpled foil and bake for 10 minutes. Take the pastry shell out of the oven and remove the foil. Lower the oven temperature to 350°F.

4 Beat together the cream, whole eggs, and egg yolks until well blended. Stir in the Parmesan and smoked salmon, and season with some salt and pepper. Pour into the pastry shell. Bake for 25 minutes until the filling is just set.

5 Carefully remove the tart from the pan and cut into slices to serve while still warm.

quattro stagioni baking-sheet tart

Family occasions often involve catering for fussy eaters, so I've based this tart on the classic "four seasons" pizza. With four different toppings, it looks pretty and should please everyone. Make two tarts for a larger gathering.

Illustrated on previous page

SERVES 4–6

17½-oz package puff pastry sheets, thawed if
   frozen
2–3 tablespoons olive oil
½ cup tomato purée
large pinch of dried oregano
5 oz mozzarella cheese, drained and diced
handful of basil leaves
sea salt and freshly ground black pepper

FOR TOPPING 1:
4 slices prosciutto, roughly torn
1 ripe fig, sliced

FOR TOPPING 2:
3–4 cremini mushrooms, thinly sliced
1 garlic clove, peeled and thinly sliced

FOR TOPPING 3:
12 slices pepperoni
1 hot red chili pepper, thinly sliced

FOR TOPPING 4:
1 tablespoon black olives
6 anchovy fillets in oil, drained

1 Preheat the oven to 425°F. Roll out the pastry to a rectangle about 16 by 10 inches and place on a baking sheet. Using a small knife, score a ½-inch border all around the edge, then prick the pastry within the border, using a fork.

2 Lightly brush the border with olive oil. Using the knife, score the rectangle into fourths. Spoon the tomato purée all over the pastry, staying with the border, then sprinkle with the oregano and some salt and pepper.

3 Arrange each topping on a fourth of the pastry, then scatter the mozzarella evenly over three of the sections, avoiding the olive and anchovy section. Drizzle with olive oil and season with salt and pepper. Bake for 20 minutes until puffed, crisp, and golden.

4 Tear the basil and scatter over, then use a pizza wheel to slice off wedges. Serve with a salad.

shrimp dupiaza with saffron rice

I have been told that dupiaza means "double onions" and is simply a basic curry. I like to give mine a touch of sweetness with coconut, and sourness with fresh lemon. I think the simple saffron rice makes a lovely partner, but plain basmati will do just fine too.

SERVES 12

3 tablespoons sunflower oil

6 onions, peeled and thinly sliced

6 cardamom pods, cracked

2¼ lb tomatoes, roughly chopped

1 cup canned coconut cream

2½ cups vegetable stock

6 tablespoons hot curry paste

1 tablespoon dark brown sugar

3 lb peeled raw tiger shrimp, thawed if frozen

grated zest and juice of 1 lemon

sea salt and freshly ground black pepper

¼ cup cilantro leaves for garnish

FOR THE RICE:

pinch of saffron threads

2 tablespoons butter

6 cups basmati rice

1 teaspoon salt

1 Preheat the oven to 350°F. Begin with the rice: Stir the saffron into 8 cups boiling water and set aside. Melt the butter in a large stovetop-to-oven casserole, add the rice, and stir to coat the grains in the butter. Cook for 1 minute, then pour in the saffron water and stir in the salt. Bring to a boil, then cover and transfer to the oven. Bake for 30 minutes until the rice is tender and the liquid has been absorbed.

2 Meanwhile, heat the oil in a roasting pan on the stovetop and cook the onions for 15 minutes until softened and golden. Add the cardamom pods and tomatoes, and cook gently for 10 minutes until the tomatoes are softened and pulpy.

3 Stir in the coconut cream, stock, curry paste, sugar, and some salt and pepper. Bring to a gentle simmer and cook for 25 minutes, adding a little water if the sauce seems too thick.

4 Stir in the shrimp with the lemon zest and juice, and cook for 2–3 minutes longer until the shrimp are just cooked.

5 Divide the rice among warm plates, spoon the curry on top (there should be plenty of sauce), and finish with a scattering of cilantro.

Asian roast chicken

This simple but flavorsome and aromatic dish looks stunning when brought to the table on a platter. You can use one very large roasting pan or two smaller ones. I like to buy whole chickens and cut them into quarters so I get a mixture of breasts and legs, plus some wings and bones to make chicken stock later. You can buy the pieces already prepared if you prefer.

SERVES 12

3 chickens, each about 4^{1}/$_{2}$ lb, quartered
4 garlic cloves, peeled and roughly chopped
4 shallots, peeled and roughly chopped
1^{1}/$_{2}$-inch piece of fresh ginger, peeled
   and roughly chopped
4 lemon grass stalks, roughly chopped
3 tablespoons light brown sugar

2 tablespoons Thai fish sauce
1^{1}/$_{4}$ cups chicken stock
juice of 1 lime
sea salt and freshly ground black pepper
6 green onions, trimmed and thinly sliced,
   for garnish

1   Deeply slash each chicken quarter two or three times and nestle them into a large roasting pan.

2   Pound the garlic, shallots, ginger, lemon grass, and 2 tablespoons of the sugar together using a mortar and pestle, to make a coarse paste. Stir in the fish sauce. Rub the mixture over the chicken pieces, making sure it goes into the slashes. Leave in a cool place for at least 2 hours (ideally overnight in the fridge), turning from time to time.

3   Preheat the oven to 400°F. Sprinkle the chicken quarters with some coarse sea salt, then roast for 45–50 minutes until beautifully crisp and brown and cooked through. Transfer to a warmed large serving platter and set aside in a warm spot to rest for 5 minutes.

4   Pour away any fat from the roasting pan, then place the pan on the stovetop and pour in the stock. Bring to a boil, stirring to loosen any residue from the bottom of the pan. Simmer for a couple of minutes, then add the lime juice and the remaining sugar, to taste.

5   Pour the sauce over the chicken, sprinkle with the green onions, and serve with rice and steamed Chinese greens.

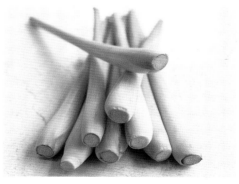

Moroccan chicken and pastina bake

Small pasta shapes are very popular in North Africa, and the addition of cinnamon, cumin, and orange gives this dish a typical Middle-Eastern flavor. It's a big, hearty family bake, and as it cooks the top of the pasta becomes golden and a little crunchy. The recipe uses a very large roasting pan, but if you don't have one, simply use two smaller pans.
Illustrated on previous page

SERVES 10

1¼ lb cherry tomatoes
10 chicken thighs
1 garlic bulb, broken into cloves
1 tablespoon olive oil
1 large red onion, peeled and thinly sliced
1½ lb conchigliette, or other tiny pasta shapes
2 cinnamon sticks, broken in half
1 teaspoon cumin seeds
8 cups hot chicken stock
grated zest and juice of 1 large orange
¼ cup chopped flat-leaf parsley
sea salt and freshly ground black pepper

1 Preheat the oven to 400°F. Put the cherry tomatoes into a large roasting pan and nestle the chicken thighs and garlic cloves among them. Drizzle with the olive oil and season with salt and pepper. Bake for 15 minutes.

2 Scatter the red onion slices over the chicken and bake for a further 5 minutes.

3 Now stir in the pasta, cinnamon, cumin, stock, orange zest and juice, and a little more seasoning. Return to the oven and bake for 15–20 minutes longer or until the pasta is cooked and the liquid has been absorbed. Stir in the chopped parsley and serve straight from the pan.

minted chicken and new potato salad

This is ideal for outdoor eating—chicken, new potatoes, and green beans tossed in a minty yogurt dressing make the perfect summer salad. Most supermarkets sell whole roasted chickens. For this recipe, I recommend you buy a plain one (rather than a flavored chicken) or, better still, roast your own, side by side in a large roasting pan.

SERVES 12

2 roast chickens, each about $3^1/_2$ lb
$3^1/_2$ lb baby new potatoes, halved if large
9 oz fine green beans, trimmed
$^1/_4$ cup pine nuts, toasted
1 bunch of green onions, trimmed and sliced
FOR THE MINTY DRESSING:
3 tablespoons thick, plain yogurt
3 tablespoons olive oil
pinch of sugar
$^1/_3$ cup mint leaves
sea salt and freshly ground black pepper

1 Remove the legs and breasts from the roast chickens. Tear the breast meat into bite-sized pieces and place in a large, wide serving bowl. Remove the leg meat from the bones and tear it into similar pieces; add to the bowl. Strip any meat from the chicken carcasses and add this too. Set aside.

2 Cook the potatoes in boiling salted water for 10–12 minutes until tender. Add the beans for the last 2–3 minutes of cooking. Drain well and cool under cold running water. Drain and pat dry on paper towels. Add to the chicken along with the pine nuts and green onions, and mix well.

3 To make the dressing, whisk together the yogurt, olive oil, 3 tablespoons water, the sugar, and some salt and pepper. Set aside a few mint leaves for garnish; mince the rest and stir into the dressing.

4 Pour the dressing over the salad, tossing to make sure everything is coated. Scatter on the reserved mint leaves and serve.

vegetable accompaniments

A vegetable accompaniment should be as flavorful and interesting as the main course. Even something like a humble baked potato can be turned into a delicious side dish—try baking whole sweet potatoes in their skins and serving with a garlic and chili butter.

We have an enormous array of vegetables available to us. Wherever possible, try to use those in season. Asparagus is available all year round now, but it's flavor when grown in a hothouse in November will never match that of fresh asparagus in March through June. In the winter months, when seasonal vegetables seem limited and boring, there are many ways to pep them up, such as stir-frying shredded cabbage with cumin seeds and toasted sesame oil, or roasting carrots with garlic. Broccoli is always popular and it's easy to liven up with a few flavorings. Each of the following accompaniments serves 4–6, but you can easily double or triple the quantities.

▲ **roasted carrots with garlic**
Scrub 1¼ lb carrots, then cut into ½-inch-thick slices. Place in a roasting pan with a splash of olive oil and a little salt and sugar. Toss to mix, then roast in the oven at 375°F for 15 minutes. Scatter a handful of whole, unpeeled garlic cloves over the carrots, and roast for 30 minutes longer until tender and golden brown. Add a splash of balsamic vinegar and some chopped parsley, then serve.

clapshot

Peel 1¼ lb each of rutabaga and russet potatoes, and cut into chunks. Boil until tender. Meanwhile, cook 2 snipped bacon slices in a frying pan until crisp and golden, then add 4 thinly sliced green onions and cook for 1 minute. Drain the rutabaga and potatoes, and mash well. Beat in the bacon and green onions, along with a splash of warm milk. Season with salt and pepper to taste and serve.

sesame, green bean, and radish salad

Blanch 1 lb fine green beans in boiling salted water for 2–3 minutes, then drain and refresh under cold running water. Sauté a thinly sliced garlic clove in 3 tbsp sunflower oil until just turning golden, then transfer to a bowl and whisk with 2 tsp toasted sesame oil and 1 tbsp light soy sauce. Combine the beans and 5 thinly sliced radishes in a serving dish and pour on the dressing. Scatter with some toasted sesame seeds and serve.

▲ broccoli with chili and lemon

Trim the base of the stem from a head of broccoli, then cut into long florets, leaving a good length of stem on each. Cook the broccoli in a pan of boiling salted water for 2 minutes, then drain. Heat a splash of sunflower oil in a nonstick frying pan and cook 1 or 2 thinly sliced garlic cloves for a few seconds. Add the broccoli and 1 or 2 sliced hot red chili peppers, and stir-fry for 2–3 minutes until tender but still firm. Squeeze in the juice of ½ lemon and season with salt and pepper. Serve hot.

succulent pork roast

This is based on a classic Italian dish known as *porchetta*. I find that shoulder of pork is the best cut to use as it has exactly the right balance of meat and fat. The pork is best served warm, but not straight from the oven.

SERVES 10–12
handful of rosemary sprigs
1 boneless pork blade roast with skin, about 9 lb
1/2 cup freshly grated Parmesan cheese
4 garlic cloves, peeled and minced
1/2 cup chopped flat-leaf parsley
sea salt and freshly ground black pepper

1   If you want the pork to have a soft, chewy skin, which is traditional for this dish, then preheat the oven now to 375°F.

2   Remove the leaves from 2 sprigs of rosemary and roughly chop. Cut the strings on the pork and open it out on a flat surface. Season generously with salt and pepper, then evenly sprinkle on the Parmesan, garlic, and chopped rosemary and parsley.

3   Roll up the pork again to enclose the filling. Tie with string at 3/4-inch intervals to keep the meat in shape. If the skin is not already scored, use a small, very sharp knife to score it between the strings. Sprinkle with salt, then slip the remaining rosemary sprigs under the strings.

4   For a soft, chewy skin, roast the pork right away, allowing 20 minutes per pound plus an extra 20 minutes— if your roast weighs 9 lb, it will take 3 hours. If you want the pork to have a crunchy skin (which will make it harder to carve), leave it for at least 2 hours before cooking. Then, before putting it in to roast, pat with paper towels to dry off the excess water. Roast at the same temperature, turning up the oven to 425°F for the last 20 minutes of the cooking time.

5   Let the pork rest for at least 30 minutes before carving. If you have an electric carving knife, it will make the carving very easy.

crusty-topped shepherd's pie

An absolute winner on any family table, this version has a little extra zing from caraway seeds, and it's topped with a delicious Cheddar mash.

SERVES 12

3 tablespoons olive oil

3 onions, peeled and chopped

4 garlic cloves, peeled and chopped

4 carrots, peeled and diced

2 teaspoons caraway seeds

3¹/₂ lb lean ground lamb

1 small head Savoy cabbage, sliced

6 cups chicken stock

6 tablespoons steak sauce

2 cups frozen green peas

³/₄ cup chopped flat-leaf parsley

FOR THE CHEDDAR MASH:

4¹/₂ lb russet or all-purpose potatoes, peeled and cubed

²/₃ cup milk

4 tablespoons butter

2 cups shredded aged Cheddar cheese

sea salt and freshly ground black pepper

1   Heat the olive oil in a large roasting pan on the stovetop. Add the onions, garlic, carrots, and caraway seeds, and cook for 3–4 minutes. Add the ground lamb and cook for 5–10 minutes longer, stirring now and again, until browned.

2   Drain off any excess fat, then stir in the cabbage and cook for another couple of minutes. Add the stock and brown sauce. Bring to a boil, then simmer very gently for 30 minutes.

3   Meanwhile, make the mash. Cook the potatoes in boiling salted water for 15–20 minutes until tender. Drain well, then mash and stir in the milk, butter, cheese, and seasoning.

4   Preheat the oven to 350°F. Stir the peas and parsley into the lamb mixture and season with salt and pepper. Spread out smoothly, then spoon the mash over the top and rough up the surface with the back of a spoon. Bake for 45 minutes until bubbling and golden.

roast shoulder of lamb with sticky pancetta potatoes

When roasting meat it's always best to have it at room temperature. So a couple of hours before roasting, take the lamb out of the fridge and dress with the marinade. For large feasts, quantities here can easily be doubled.

SERVES 6–8

1 whole shoulder of lamb, about 5$^1/_2$ lb
2 garlic cloves, peeled and minced
$^1/_4$ cup minced mint
1 teaspoon dried oregano
3 tablespoons olive oil
3$^1/_2$–4$^1/_2$ lb red-skinned potatoes, scrubbed
4 oz cubed pancetta (Italian bacon)
2 red onions, thinly sliced
$^1/_2$ cup hard cider
sea salt and freshly ground black pepper

1 Place the lamb on a rack set over a roasting pan. Using a skewer, deeply pierce the meat in several places. Stir together the garlic, mint, oregano, olive oil, and some salt and pepper. Brush all over the lamb, then set aside for at least an hour.

2 Preheat the oven to 400°F. Cook the whole potatoes in a pan of boiling salted water for about 15 minutes. Drain, then cut into ¾-inch-thick slices.

3 Lift the lamb on its rack off the roasting pan, and scatter the sliced potatoes, pancetta, and red onion into the pan. Season with salt and pepper and pour the cider over. Replace the rack and roast the lamb for 1 hour 35 minutes.

4 Transfer the lamb to a warm platter and let rest in a warm spot for 15 minutes before carving. In the meantime, turn the oven off and put the pan of potatoes back in to keep warm. Serve the lamb with the sticky pancetta potatoes.

boiled beef and carrots with herb dumplings

This is a proper old-fashioned English stew with suet dumplings. I've chosen to use lard as the cooking fat, but if you prefer you can substitute a couple of tablespoons of vegetable oil. I don't have a casserole big enough, so I use a deep, heavy roasting pan. If you happen to have a very large stovetop-to-oven casserole, do use it.

SERVES 10

3 tablespoons lard
4¹/₂ lb chuck steak, cut into large cubes
¹/₄ cup all-purpose flour
4 onions, peeled and sliced
3¹/₄ lb carrots, peeled and thickly sliced
2 bay leaves
3 rosemary sprigs
2 cups red wine
6 cups hot beef stock
sea salt and freshly ground black pepper

FOR THE DUMPLINGS:
1³/₄ cups self-rising flour
1 teaspoon baking powder
¹/₂ teaspoon salt
¹/₂ heaped cup shredded beef suet
¹/₄ cup minced flat-leaf parsley or chives

1 Preheat the oven to 325°F. Set the roasting pan on the stovetop and add the lard to melt.

2 Meanwhile, toss the meat in the flour to coat lightly. Add to the pan and cook for 10 minutes, stirring frequently, until nicely browned. Remove and set aside.

3 Add the onions to the roasting pan and brown them, then add the carrots, bay leaves, rosemary, wine, and stock. Return the browned beef and add some seasoning. Bring to a boil. Cover with foil and transfer to the oven to cook for 2 hours until the meat is tender.

4 To make the dumplings, place the flour in a large bowl and stir in the baking powder, salt, suet, and herbs. Stir in enough water—about ²/₃ cup—to make a soft dough. Don't worry if it's a little sticky. Roll into 20 balls, each about the size of a cherry.

5 Drop the dumplings into the stew and continue cooking in the oven, still covered, for 30–35 minutes until the dumplings are puffed and cooked through.

7 desserts

lemonade granita

This is the perfect do-ahead dessert. The balance of sugar, acidic lemon, and water means that it freezes into a beautifully textured granita. It will keep in the freezer for weeks, but may then need a firm hand to break up the crystals.
Illustrated left

SERVES 6
1 cup sugar
grated zest and juice of 6 lemons
1 lemon grass stalk, roughly flattened with a
   rolling pin
2 cups soda water

1   Put the sugar, lemon zest and juice, and lemon grass stalk into a saucepan with ¾ cup water. Heat gently, stirring, until the sugar dissolves, then simmer gently for 5 minutes. Let cool.

2   Strain the liquid into a rigid container and stir in the soda water. Freeze for 2 hours until almost firm, then use a fork to break the mixture into large, flaky crystals. Freeze for 2 hours longer, then break up again. Spoon into small glasses for serving.

frozen berry-yogurt pots

A simple fruit ice with nuggets of melt-in-the-mouth meringue, this is incredibly easy to prepare.
Illustrated on page 95

MAKES 6
¾ cup confectioners' sugar
2 cups frozen summer berries
¼ cup black-currant or blackberry syrup
2 cups thick, plain yogurt
2 large baked meringue shells, crumbled

1   Sift the confectioners' sugar over the frozen fruit, then drizzle on the black-currant syrup. Roughly break up the fruit with a fork.

2   Tip the yogurt into a bowl and beat with a wooden spoon to soften. Ripple through the fruit mixture along with the crumbled meringues.

3   Spoon into 6 small, freezerproof glasses and freeze for 2–3 hours until firm. If you freeze for longer than this, take the pots out of the freezer 10–20 minutes before serving, to soften up.

Bellini gelatins

Here, the classic Venetian cocktail is made into a gently wobbling dessert. Make ahead and serve as the ultimate dinner party finale, or between courses as a palate-cleanser.

SERVES 6

2½ cups dry white wine

1 cup sugar

5 sheets of leaf gelatin

1 large peach

¼ cup peach schnapps or peach brandy

1 pink rose

1 Place the wine and sugar in a small pan and simmer gently, stirring, until the sugar dissolves.

2 Meanwhile, soak the gelatin leaves in a shallow dish of cold water until softened, then drain and squeeze out the excess water. Remove the wine from the heat, add the gelatin leaves, and stir until melted. Set aside to cool.

3 Cut a cross in the skin at the base of the peach, then plunge into boiling water. Leave for 1 minute, then remove. Using a small knife, peel off all the skin. Halve, remove the pit, and roughly chop the flesh. Purée in a mini chopper until smooth, then press through a strainer.

4 Once the wine is at room temperature, stir in the peach purée and schnapps, then pour into 6 molds or ramekins. Carefully pull some of the petals from the rose and float a couple of rose petals on each gelatin. Chill for at least 3 hours until set.

5 To serve, dip the molds briefly into hot water, then turn out the gelatins onto small plates. Decorate with more rose petals (and the rosebud, if you like).

little apricot and lavender mousses

Make these light-as-air fruit mousses in early summer when fragrant fresh apricots are in season.

SERVES 6

2¼ lb apricots, pitted and roughly chopped

⅔ cup sugar

½ teaspoon lavender flowers or 2 rosemary sprigs

1 sheet of leaf gelatin

1 egg white

⅔ cup heavy cream

1   Combine the apricots, sugar, lavender, and 5 tablespoons water in a saucepan. Cook gently for 15–20 minutes, stirring from time to time, until the fruit is pulpy and almost smooth.

2   Soak the leaf gelatin in a shallow dish of cold water until softened, then drain and squeeze out the excess water. Remove the apricot mixture from the heat and stir in the leaf gelatin until melted. Let cool. (If you used rosemary in place of the lavender, remove the sprig at this stage.)

3   Beat the egg white until it forms firm peaks. Whip the cream in another bowl until thick. Fold the egg white and cream into the cooled apricot mixture. Spoon into individual pots or glasses and chill for at least 2 hours until set.

coffee cream trifle

This simple trifle needs a night in the fridge, so it's perfect as a make-ahead dinner party dessert. Overnight the sugar melts into the cream, leaving a scrumptious syrupy layer on the surface.

SERVES 8

5 oz cantuccini (small Italian biscotti)

½ cup strong black coffee

¼ cup sweet Marsala or other sweet wine

1¼ cups heavy cream

2 cups thick, plain yogurt

6 tablespoons coarse raw sugar (Demerara or
   Turbinado)

1   Break the cantuccini roughly into a glass serving bowl. Pour the coffee and Marsala over them. Let soak for 10 minutes or so.

2   Meanwhile, whip the cream until it forms soft peaks, then stir in the yogurt. Spoon this mixture over the cantuccini and sprinkle the sugar on top. Cover and chill overnight.

panettone bruschetta with summer fruit compote

This most spectacular summer dessert of sugar-toasted slices of panettone topped with juicy berries can double as a brilliant breakfast.

SERVES 4

2/3 *cup freshly squeezed orange juice*

1 vanilla bean, halved lengthwise

1 star anise

1/4 *cup granulated sugar*

3 cups mixed summer berries, such as
  raspberries, strawberries, and blueberries

4 large slices of panettone

4 tablespoons butter, melted

2 tablespoons confectioners' sugar

4 tablespoons thick, plain yogurt or crème
  fraîche

1 Heat the orange juice in a small pan with the split vanilla bean, star anise, and confectioners' sugar. Bring to a gentle boil, then remove from the heat. Stir in the fruit and let cool completely, then chill until ready to serve.

2 Preheat a ridged grill pan. Brush the panettone with the melted butter, then dust with confectioners' sugar. Toast on the grill pan for 1–2 minutes on each side until crisp and golden brown.

3 Divide the grilled panettone among four plates and spoon the fruit compote on top, discarding the vanilla bean and star anise. Add a spoonful of yogurt to each portion and serve.

effortless desserts

Most of us like a little something sweet at the end of a meal, but without a lot of fuss. When a piece of fruit just isn't enough, or when you've planned a busy dinner party and want to save time on the dessert, make good use of simple ingredients and quality convenience foods. With these you can turn out an impressive and satisfying dessert in a matter of minutes.

Stir together creamy ingredients such as mascarpone or softly whipped cream with strawberries mashed with confectioners' sugar, to make a speedy fruit fool. This needs only a shortbread cookie alongside.

Many fruits, including rhubarb, plums, and peaches, can be baked to good effect: dot with a little butter and add a sprinkling of sugar and spice, then bake until tender (up to 30 minutes, depending on the fruit you choose). Serve with a scoop of vanilla ice cream or a dollop of crème fraîche. Or, try one of the following speedy ideas.

▲ **raspberry slush**
To serve 4, put 2 cups frozen raspberries into a food processor with ¼ cup sweetened lime juice and 1 cup fizzy lemonade. Blend to form a coarse slush. Pour into glasses and serve immediately.

stir-fried toffee pineapple

To serve 3–4, drain 15 oz canned pineapple chunks and pat dry on paper towels. Heat 1 tbsp butter in a frying pan and add the pineapple, 2 tbsp light brown sugar, and 2 tbsp dried shredded coconut. Cook over a high heat for 4–5 minutes until golden brown. Serve immediately, with scoops of vanilla ice cream.

chocolate-banana cups

To serve 6, melt 7 oz (7 squares) bittersweet chocolate in the microwave or in a bowl set over a pan of simmering water. Pour 2 cups prepared vanilla pudding into a large bowl and, using an electric mixer, gradually beat in the chocolate until smooth and well blended. Stir in 2 chopped bananas, then pour into 6 cups or glasses. If you have time, place in the fridge to chill and set.

▲ fluffy blueberry pancakes

To serve 4, whisk together 2 eggs and 5 tbsp milk. Combine 1 cup all-purpose flour, 2 tbsp sugar, and a pinch of salt in a large bowl. Make a well in the center, pour in the egg mixture, and whisk until smooth. Stir in 1 cup blueberries. Heat just a tiny splash of sunflower oil in a nonstick pan. Add spoonfuls of the batter and cook for 1–2 minutes on each side until puffed and golden. Stack and sprinkle with confectioners' sugar. Serve with maple syrup and cream.

strawberry clafoutis

Although this is an incredibly simple dessert, it looks very stylish, which makes it perfect for entertaining. The idea came from my friend, chef Paul Merret, who makes this with juicy fresh peach cubes. I love to eat warm clafoutis topped with a scoop of melting ice cream.
Illustrated on previous page

SERVES 4
4 eggs
3/4 cup sugar
2/3 cup heavy cream
1 tablespoon all-purpose flour
1 tablespoon ground almonds
grated zest of 1 lime
8 oz strawberries, halved if large

1   Preheat the oven to 375°F. Using an electric mixer, beat the eggs with the sugar until really thick and voluminous.

2   Lightly whip the cream until it forms soft peaks. Fold the cream into the egg mixture along with the flour, ground almonds, and lime zest.

3   Divide the strawberries among four heatproof bowls or individual gratin dishes. Spoon the batter over the berries. Bake for 12 minutes until golden. Serve warm, each clafoutis topped with a scoop of vanilla ice cream.

melting chocolate risotto

What could be better than rice pudding? Chocolate rice pudding! This one's an absolute stunner.

SERVES 6

3 cups milk

1/4 cup packed light brown sugar

4 tablespoons butter

1/2 teaspoon ground cinnamon

1/2 cup risotto rice, such as Carnaroli
  or Arborio

4 oz (4 squares) bittersweet chocolate,
  roughly chopped

1 Put the milk and brown sugar into a pan and heat gently until the sugar dissolves.

2 Melt the butter in a large nonstick pan and stir in the cinnamon and rice. Cook for 1 minute, then add half of the hot sugared milk. Cook for 10 minutes, stirring from time to time. Pour in the remaining hot milk, and stir and cook for 8–10 minutes longer until the rice is tender and the milk has been absorbed.

3 Scatter the chocolate over the pudding and stir to ripple through roughly. Spoon into bowls and serve warm. Alternatively, spoon into glasses and chill before serving.

soggy-belly chocolate fudge cake

Here is a fabulous cross between a classic chocolate cake and a fudgy brownie. It is best eaten on the day it's made, while still warm, which shouldn't be too much trouble. Serve with cream or vanilla ice cream.

SERVES 8

7 oz (7 squares) bittersweet chocolate

9 tablespoons butter

3 tablespoons Irish cream liqueur or whiskey

5 eggs, separated

1 cup vanilla-flavored superfine sugar or plain superfine sugar

2/3 cup all-purpose flour

1 teaspoon baking powder

1 Preheat the oven to 350°F. Line a 9-inch springform cake pan with parchment paper.

2 Put the chocolate, butter, and liqueur into a large heatproof bowl set over a pan of gently simmering water and heat until melted. Remove from the heat and let cool for a couple of minutes. Stir until smooth.

3 Meanwhile, beat the egg whites in a clean bowl until they form soft peaks. Gradually beat in the sugar, a tablespoonful at a time.

4 Stir the eggs yolks into the chocolate mixture, then fold in the beaten egg white mixture. Sift the flour and baking powder over the surface and gently fold in using a large metal spoon.

5 Pour the batter into the prepared pan and bake for 30–40 minutes until just set. Let cool in the pan for at least 20 minutes, then gently lift out of the pan and cut into wedges to serve.

best ever vanilla cheesecake

Most cheesecakes are good, but, with its fantastic texture and light lemon and vanilla flavor, this one is unbeatable. Keep it in the fridge and cut slices off it all week.

SERVES 10

2 cups crushed gingersnap cookies
4 tablespoons butter, melted
1 vanilla bean
3 cups mascarpone cheese
$2/3$ cup sugar
2 tablespoons cornstarch
3 eggs
grated zest of 1 lemon

1   Preheat the oven to 350°F. Stir the cookie crumbs with the melted butter until evenly mixed. Turn the crumb mixture into a 9-inch nonstick springform cake pan and press down firmly with the back of a spoon. Chill for 5–10 minutes.

2   Using a small knife, slit open the vanilla bean and scrape the seeds into a large bowl. Add the mascarpone, sugar, cornstarch, eggs, and lemon zest, and beat with an electric mixer until smooth.

3   Pour the mixture into the cake pan and set on a baking sheet. Bake for 45 minutes or until golden —the filling will still be a little wobbly at this stage. Turn off the oven, open the door, and leave the cheesecake inside until completely cool—the filling will set as it cools. Cut into wedges to serve.

snowy saffron peaches

Roasting really brings out the natural sweetness of ripe peaches. The snowy saffron meringues finish them off with a stylish flourish. Serve with vanilla ice cream.

SERVES 6

4 tablespoons butter

6 large, ripe peaches, halved

1 tablespoon roughly chopped pistachio nuts

⅓ cup superfine sugar

small pinch of saffron threads

1 egg white

1 Preheat the oven to 400°F. Melt the butter in a small roasting pan in the oven, then put in the peach halves in one layer. Scatter in the nuts. Roast for 25 minutes, turning from time to time, until the peaches are tender and golden.

2 Meanwhile, blend the sugar with the saffron in a mini chopper or blender. Beat the egg white in a clean bowl to stiff peaks, then gradually beat in the saffron sugar to make a firm, glossy meringue.

3 Turn the peach halves hollow side up. Spoon a peak of meringue on top of each one. Return to the oven to bake for 5 minutes until lightly tinged with brown. Serve hot, with the pan juices and nuts drizzled around.

syrup tart

Could there possibly be a better accompaniment to a cup of afternoon tea than this? The sweetness of the syrup and the zesty bite of lemon never fail to please.

SERVES 10

1²/₃ cups all-purpose flour

10 tablespoons cold butter, diced

1 egg yolk

1 teaspoon sugar

FOR THE FILLING:

2¹/₂ cups golden syrup

3 cups fresh white bread crumbs

finely grated zest of 2 lemons

²/₃ cup rolled oats

2 eggs, beaten

1 Preheat the oven to 350°F. Put the flour and butter into a food processor and pulse until the mixture forms fine crumbs. Add the egg yolk, sugar, and 2 tablespoons cold water, and pulse again briefly until the mixture comes together into a dough.

2 Roll out the dough on a lightly floured surface and use to line a fluted, deep, loose-bottomed 9¹/₂-inch tart pan. Prick the bottom and chill for 30 minutes.

3 To make the filling, warm the golden syrup in a pan until runny but not too hot. Remove from the heat and stir in the bread crumbs, lemon zest, oats, and beaten eggs.

4 Pour the filling into the pastry shell. Bake for 30–40 minutes until the filling is golden and just set; don't worry if it is still a little soft. Let cool in the pan for a few minutes, then carefully lift out. Cut into slices to serve.

old-fashioned coconut tart

A wonderful moist tart, this has a layer of red jelly between the pastry and coconut filling. It beats any similar tart I've ever eaten.

SERVES 8

13 oz refrigerated piecrust dough

3 eggs

²⁄₃ cup sugar

1 cup canned coconut cream

1 cup unsweetened shredded dried coconut

¹⁄₂ cup all-purpose flour

¹⁄₄ cup raspberry jelly

1   Preheat the oven to 400°F. Roll out the dough on a lightly floured surface and use to line a fluted, deep, loose-bottomed 9¹⁄₂-inch tart pan. If you have time, let rest in the fridge for 30 minutes. Prick the pastry shell lightly with a fork, fill with crumpled foil, and bake for 15 minutes until set.

2   Using an electric mixer, beat the eggs and sugar together until thick and voluminous. Gently stir in the coconut cream, shredded coconut, and flour.

3   Reduce the oven temperature to 350°F. Lift the foil out of the pastry shell, then spread the jelly over the bottom. Pour in the coconut mixture.

4   Bake for 30–40 minutes until the filling is set and golden. Let cool in the pan for a few minutes, then carefully lift out, slice, and serve.

oaty ginger-pear crisp

A crisp is one of the easiest and most comforting desserts ever made. The stem ginger in this filling gives every mouthful a little zing.

SERVES 8

8 pears
4 tablespoons butter
1/4 cup packed light brown sugar
4 pieces of stem ginger in syrup, drained
  and minced
juice of 1 lemon
FOR THE CRISP TOPPING:
10 tablespoons (11/4 sticks) cold butter, diced
2 cups all-purpose flour
11/4 cups rolled oats
3/4 cup packed light brown sugar

1 Preheat the oven to 350°F. Peel, quarter, and core the pears, then cut into chunks. Put the butter into a pan with the pears, sugar, ginger, and lemon juice, and cook gently for 10 minutes.

2 Meanwhile, make the crisp topping. Rub the butter into the flour until there are no large pieces left. Stir in the oats and sugar.

3 Spoon the fruit mixture into a large baking dish and scatter the crisp mixture over the top. Bake for 40–45 minutes until nicely browned. Serve with hot custard sauce.

index

Acknowledgments
First, thanks to all my family and friends for tasting each and every one of the dishes in this book. Special thanks to everyone involved in the production of the book, to Anna-Lisa for her careful testing, great suggestions, and help with preparing the food for photography; Gus, Vanessa, and Will for making the book look so beautiful; and Janet for putting the whole thing together. I am especially grateful to Jane and Alison at Quadrille for their confidence in me. And, last but not least, thanks to my favorite girls at Fork, my agents Sarah and Jerry, and my champion-taster—the handsome Roberto.